Great Southern Mysteries

Great Southern Mysteries

E. Randall Floyd

August House / Little Rock
PUBLISHERS

Printed in the United States of America

10 9 8 7 6 5 4 3

LIBRARY OF CONGRESS CATALOGING-IN-PUBLICATION DATA

Great Southern Mysteries / (collected by) E. Randall Floyd.—1st ed.
p.
cm.
Bibliography: p.
Includes index.
ISBN 0-87483-097-4: $16.95
1. Southern States—History, Local.
2. Curiosities and wonders—Southern States.
3. Legends—Southern States. I. Floyd, E. Randall
F209.5.G74 1989   89-33593
002.9' 4' 0975—dc20   CIP
First paperback edition 1991

Cover illustration by Byron Taylor
Production artwork by Ira Hocut
Typography by Lettergraphics, Memphis, Tennessee
Design direction by Ted Parkhurst
Project direction by Hope Coulter

This book is printed on archival-quality paper which meets the
guidelines for performance and durability of the Committee on
Production Guidelines for Book Longevity of the Council on
Library Resources.

AUGUST HOUSE, INC.   PUBLISHERS   LITTLE ROCK

This book is for Uncle Curt, who taught me the magic of words;
for my mother, who waited so long;
for Selma, who wouldn't let me give up;
and for Anne, who stayed by my side.

Contents

Fabled Lands And Vanished Peoples

Blue-Eyed Savages and Talking Books

EUROPEAN SETTLERS PUSHING inland along the rugged Lumber River in the eighteenth century were surprised to discover a tribe of English-speaking Indians who dressed like white frontiersmen and lived in remarkably comfortable houses. Even more astounding was the way many of these strange "savages" looked. Although most had dark skins, a few were fair-complexioned and had blond hair and blue eyes. Some could even read, claiming white gods had long ago taught their ancestors how to "talk in books," which, the explorers understood, meant to read and write.

Today the descendants of that mysterious group of people are known as the Lumbees, and they still inhabit the same harsh region of North Carolina where they were discovered more than two centuries ago. Since they were one of the largest groups of Indians in the United States, it is ironic that few people outside the states of North Carolina and Virginia have ever heard of them. The reason, according to scholars, is that at some time in the remote past the Lumbees apparently lost their own language and cultural identity. While cultural and linguistic traditions continued to flourish among better known southeastern tribes, such as the Cherokees, Choctaws, and Creeks, the heritage of the Lumbees became obscure.

Who were these blue-eyed Indians, and how did their ancestors learn to "talk in books"? One intriguing theory is that the estimated forty thousand modern Lumbees are descended from the survivors of Sir Walter Raleigh's lost colony of Roanoke, which vanished without a trace in 1589 along with more than a hundred men, women, and children. The settlement was the brainchild of Sir Walter Raleigh, a dashing, daring, and somewhat reckless consort of Queen Elizabeth who, along with his older brother—Sir Humphrey Gilbert, a famed explorer and soldier of fortune—sought adventure and wealth in the newly discovered lands beyond the great sea. In 1584 Raleigh asked for and received a charter to explore the southern coast of the New World, with the intention of setting up a buffer colony in the path of advancing Spanish settlers. Raleigh's reconnoitering force made landfall two thousand miles south of New Foundland and spent the next month exploring the dark, unfriendly coast south of Chesapeake Bay.

One year later Raleigh outfitted an expedition to settle Roanoke Island, a remote wooded isle near the present boundary between Virginia and North Carolina. The settlement failed, however, mainly because of the colonists' preoccupation with finding gold rather than tending fields. Unfriendly natives also influenced their decision to abandon the colony that summer and to return to England by hitching a ride with Sir Francis Drake, fresh from piratical raids in the West Indies.

In spite of tremendous personal financial losses with the first expedition, Raleigh was determined to send another group of colonists, this time about 130 persons under the command of John White, who in time would become famous for his early drawings of colonial life in North America. White spent about a month getting the new settlement started, then returned to England for fresh supplies. Among the settlers he left behind were his daughter, her husband, and their newborn daughter, Virginia Dare (believed to be the first child of European parents born in the New World). Before departing, he left strict instructions that should the remaining colonists be forced to leave the settlement in his absence, they were to inscribe their destination in a "conspicuous place."

As fate would have it, war broke out with Spain later that year and White was unable to return to the colony on schedule. The entire Spanish fleet had attacked England, forcing every available ship into military service. Not until 1590—two years later—was the war-weary governor able to return to his settlement, three thousand miles away from the bloody battle-fields and bays of Europe.

It was a grim sight that awaited White upon his arrival at Roanoke. Not only had the settlement been ransacked and destroyed, but the entire population had vanished—every man, woman, and child, including his daughter and baby granddaughter. In vain the grief-stricken governor searched the island for signs of their fate. The only clue to the where-abouts of the settlers was a single word carved into a wooden post—"Croatan." White finally decided that the colonists must have abandoned Roanoke when supplies ran out and made their way to nearby Hatteras. Although he conducted a lim-ited search for the settlers, bad weather and pressing royal obligations back in England forced him to leave fairly soon. Why he never returned or at least ordered a full-scale investi-gation into the colonists' disappearance has never been fully explained.

Historians still argue over the meaning of "Croatan." That was the name of an island south of Roanoke, known to have been inhabited by the friendly Hatteras tribe. Nevertheless, some researchers believe it was the name of an Indian tribe that attacked the settlement and killed the colonists. They say that after the massacre the settlers may have been cannibal-ized, since no trace of their bones or belongings has been found. Other experts theorize that most of the settlers proba-bly starved to death or died of unknown diseases. Hostile Indians could have done away with any survivors, or simply carried off some of the women and children into slavery. Charles Hudson, a University of Georgia anthropologist and author of *The Southeastern Indians,* suggests that Roanoke's settlers simply joined up with a local Indian tribe in order to survive. Still others speculate they were hauled off by pirates—even though there were no known pirates operating in those waters at the time—while at least one researcher believes the colonists were kidnapped by extraterrestrials.

A number of scholars believe it is possible that the survivors of Roanoke reached the Croatan island and intermarried with the Hatteras. This is the most reasonable explanation for the sudden disappearance of the Roanoke settlers, the one most widely accepted by historians of that period, and the one held by Governor White at the time. Researchers studying the modern Lumbees point to that group's blue eyes, blond hair, and fair complexions as lingering proof of their ancestral contact with the Europeans at Roanoke. The Lumbees themselves insist they are descended from the Roanoke colony, and there is additional evidence to indicate their claim might be justified. Of the 95 surnames of the lost colonists of Roanoke— names such as Sampson, Cooper, and Dare—no fewer than forty-one can be found among the Lumbees.

Starting in about 1650 many Hatteras Indians migrated to the mainland, settling in the Lumber River Valley. And when the first whites reached the wild hinterland of the Lumber River swamps in the late eighteenth century, the Indians they encountered wore handsome, European-style clothing, lived in multi-room dwellings, and were familiar with the English language. They were also familiar with whiskey and displayed drinking habits hauntingly reminiscent of sixteenth-century Europeans. When asked to identify themselves, these Indians said they were "Croatans"—the same name Governor White had found carved on the wooden palisade in 1590.

The Mystifying Melungeons

WHEN EUROPEANS FIRST settled the southern United States, Indians were considered savages, little better than animals. Some explorers were not even convinced that Indians were human at all. If God had created a place for them in his great cosmic scheme, then why hadn't he bothered to mention them in the Bible, his own Holy Word?

Later, as more and more whites poured into the once remote valleys and plains of the southern Appalachian wilderness, conflict with the original inhabitants became inevitable. The "subhuman" status of the Indians was reason enough for gold-hungry settlers to justify gobbling up lands, ransacking forests, and massacring any natives who got in the way.

Then came the nineteenth century, when some conscience-smitten Europeans and Americans began looking upon the "Red Man" as a kind of "noble savage," descended, certainly, from proud European or Near Eastern stock. How else could they account for the dazzling stone pyramids in the jungles of Central America and the enormous earthen monuments scattered throughout the southeastern United States and Mississippi Valley? Where else could native Americans have learned the technology required to erect such striking structures? How could their intricate cultures, no matter how paganized and vulgar, have developed without assistance and cultural influences from advanced civilizations beyond the sea?

These and other troubling questions were on the minds of many eighteenth- and nineteenth-century historians, archae-

14

ologists, and clergymen as they roamed the southern frontier. The birth of archaeology in the nineteenth century, and particularly discoveries made in Egypt and other areas of the Middle East, only enlarged rather than resolved these questions. For a time it was thought that the American Indians were descended from—or at least related to—the Romans, Carthaginians, Libyans, Chinese, Basques, Iberians, and even the Irish. The nineteenth century saw the rise of theories that survivors from the lost continent of Atlantis had reached the New World, mingling with local Indians along the southern coast and eventually masterminding construction of the pyramids on both sides of the Atlantic. Thus they supposedly imported the advanced technologies that enabled the savage Indians to rise from their Stone Age culture.

Today, despite increasingly accurate means of analyzing evidence, the origins of native Americans still inspire elaborate theorizing—from Gladwyn's belief that part of the fleet of Alexander the Great brought civilization to southern waters, to Erich von Daniken's proposition that beings from outer space engendered the human race. However, in spite of more than four centuries of speculation and research, no conclusive evidence supports any theory linking prehistoric America with trans-Atlantic, extraterrestrial, or Atlantean contacts.

In Hancock County, Tennessee, along the rugged Virginia border high in the southern Appalachian mountains, there lives a group whose uncertain origins are a prime example of the controversy. Intelligent and quiet, they are known locally as the Melungeons—perhaps because of their curious mixture of ethnic traits, or *mélange,* which includes reddish-copper skin, straight, fair hair, thin lips, and narrow faces.

Some scholars think the Melungeons are the grandchildren of shipwrecked Portuguese sailors who intermarried with their coastal ancestors. Others believe they may be descended in part from Spanish soldiers who deserted Hernando De Soto's army in the sixteenth century. Yet another explanation is that the Melungeons might be descended from the so-called

Ten Lost Tribes of Israel. That theory has also been used to account for the bewildering accomplishments of other native American civilizations, most notably the Aztecs of Mexico, the Mayans of Central America, and even the Incas of Peru. Some scholars see physical and cultural links between these Old and New World societies, pointing to architectural, religious, artistic, and linguistic similarities. It has also been posited that the Melungeons' ancestors were Mayans, Moors (thought to have sailed to America during the American Revolution), or Phoenicians, an ancient race of seafarers. Or perhaps the clan is descended from one or two Indians or blacks who intermarried locally. Thus they would be of very recent origin, perhaps late colonial or even antebellum times.

And who do the Melungeons themselves say they are? They claim to be descended from survivors of Sir Walter Raleigh's ill-fated colony on Roanoke Island in North Carolina. They are a reclusive people, mostly farmers, preferring the lonely hills and simple village life to the razzle-dazzle of modern society. They have a rich store of folktales and excel in the telling of tall tales. Their ancestors, they say, migrated to the mountains from a "land at the edge of the great sea," bringing with them unusual customs and traditions that resembled those of Europeans at the time of the North American conquest.

The Riddle of the Mounds

WHEN THE FIRST Spanish explorers reached North America, they were surprised to find tens of thousands of huge, pyramid-shaped mounds of earth dotting the landscape from Louisiana to Virginia. At first they were intrigued by these strange artificial hills, many of which towered above the dark virgin forests and mosquito-infested river valleys. As they probed deeper into the wilderness, they couldn't help but wonder who had built—and apparently abandoned—the massive earthenworks. Certainly not the primitive natives. It had to be somebody else—some powerful, long-vanished race of people. But the Spanish, lured on by prospects of finding gold and silver, never really bothered to ponder the mysteries of the mounds. That challenge was left up to a new wave of Europeans arriving on the scene—the English.

During the 1600s and 1700s, numerous reports trickled back to the British colonies about earthen structures dominating the landscape of several southern states. It is now thought that over 100,000 American mounds existed at the time of the Europeans' arrival. They came in all shapes and sizes, from low heaps of earth sculpted into the shapes of giant birds, people, and real or mythological animals, to great geometrically shaped pyramids with steep, well-graded slopes and flat tops accessible by ramps. There were so many mounds in some areas that they could only be appreciated from the air— an odd distinction in the era before airplanes.

In some ways these hillocks rival anything built by the

ancient Egyptians or the Meso-American cultures of Central and South America. At one mound site called Poverty Point in northern Louisiana, it has been determined that some 530,000 cubic yards of earth were used in erecting a single mound. Over three million man-hours of labor were expended during the project, according to James A. Ford and C.H. Webb, two archaeologists who have studied the site thoroughly.

Another important mound complex was located along the banks of the Ocmulgee River near Macon, Georgia. Ocmulgee's origins date back several thousand years and probably preceded another powerful southeastern group that developed an equally dazzling culture on the banks of the Etowah River near Cartersville, Georgia. Like mound complexes located elsewhere in the Southeast, the Georgia sites were dominated by a group of major mounds surrounded by several smaller hills and underground ceremonial chambers.

A third mound site, located on a plateau by the Black Warrior River near Tuscaloosa, Alabama, consisted of a palisaded area covering about three hundred acres with twenty platform mounds (the largest of which rises almost sixty feet) and a 7.5-acre plaza. This settlement, known as Moundville, was believed to have been built more than a thousand years ago. In time it became one of the most powerful city-states in the Southeast, controlling a territory of more than 250 square miles.

Small wonder that pioneers coming upon the grand monuments were hard-pressed for explanations. But their curiosity was only piqued further when they tried to inquire. Although a few of the mounds were still in use when the Europeans arrived, not even the native Americans themselves knew the origins of the older mounds. When questioned by advancing colonists about the earthenworks, the customary explanation was that they had been built long ago, in the dim past, ages before the present era.

These explanations were all that was needed for the overactive imagination of most European-Americans to link the mounds with some legendary ancient race, some enormously superior civilization that had flowered and vanished in remote antiquity. Like their Spanish predecessors, European and American travelers thought it impossible that the primitive tribes they encountered were capable of such engineering and technological marvels.

For years the controversy raged, pitting one school of experts against another. Cotton Mather, the fiery preacher and witch-hunter from Boston, had a simple answer. In 1702 he asserted that the devil had brought the "Red Men" to America and that they were not the architects of the mounds. That credit had to go to some other group of people, perhaps ancient Europeans who had settled the wild American shores at some time in the distant past.

Thomas Jefferson may have been the first American seriously to ponder the meaning of the enigmatic mounds. He did so while conducting the world's first scientific "dig" on his farm in Virginia. Using his own methodology for tunneling through a large mound on his property, Jefferson carefully recorded the recovery of bones and artifacts by layer—a system that would in time be adopted by archaeologists the world over. Jefferson wrote about his excavation in a small book entitled *Notes on Virginia.* The book proved immensely popular, both among scholars and lay people, and served to ignite considerable interest in American antiquities.

Others responded to the mounds in different ways. They theorized that the builders of the mounds might have come from Atlantis, the mythological continent that supposedly sank beneath the sea during a cataclysmic upheaval between ten and fifty thousand years ago. Survivors of that disaster could have reached North America, intermingled with natives there, and helped them advance culturally.

The ancient Egyptians also figure prominently in early trans-oceanic theories. Stories began circulating in the late 1700s and throughout the 1800s that Egyptian, Phoenician, and Libyan traders crossed the Atlantic regularly on international trading expeditions. Naturally they could have lent a technological hand to the New World "savages."

In time even wilder theories emerged. Colonel James Churchward in 1931 announced that he had finally solved the riddle of the mounds. According to Churchward, who believed mankind originated on a legendary land mass located in the Pacific Ocean called Mu, "The oldest records of man are not to be found in Egypt or the Valley of the Euphrates, but right here in North America and in the Orient where Mu planted her first colonies!"

Modern archaeologists cringe at the word "mound-builder," since in their view there was not just one people responsible for the earthen structures. Instead, numerous groups of Indians contributed to the mound-building tradition through the centuries—a tradition which probably had already ended before the arrival of the first Europeans. The people who built the mounds in Mississippi, Louisiana, Virginia, Georgia, Tennessee, Alabama, Florida, and the Carolinas were the ancestors of modern Indians.

In spite of the large number of mounds scattered throughout the Southeast, surprisingly few Americans know they exist. Their ignorance is probably due to the fact that until a few years ago native American history was conspicuously absent from school textbooks. Nowadays, interest in America's pre-colonial past continues to grow. Hundreds of new books and films about ancient America attest to the country's new love affair with pre-Columbian times. Perhaps it will be only a matter of time before we can satisfactorily close the book on the mystery of the great earthen mounds.

The World Within

TENS OF THOUSANDS of years ago, our ancestors moved into caves to protect themselves from the elements and other dangers of the outside world. Not only did caves serve as homes, but also they took on importance as ceremonial and religious chambers, places where people could go to communicate quietly and directly with their gods. Most of these sacred realms were probably hidden away from the rest of the cave— dank recesses where silence and flickering shadows helped worshippers get closer to the spirit world.

Over time, such subterranean worlds began to seize the human imagination, and tortured fantasies were constructed to help account for boiling lakes of fire found in volcanoes and vast, beast-filled hollows and caverns beneath mountains and hills. During the age of exploration and discovery, adventurers began descending into formerly forbidden realms to poke, probe, and ponder the mysteries within. Invariably these were places said to be haunted by giants, devils, evil dwarfs, prehistoric monsters, and a nightmarish array of other unholy horrors. Occasionally stories were published in newspapers about the discovery of lost worlds far below the earth, or of lost civilizations inhabited by advanced peoples. These stories became embellished over the years. Somewhere along the way, these netherlands became associated with death and demons, with dragons and the supernatural—an association that prevails even in our high-tech age. Even as the human mind developed and reached far out to the stars, it never forgot the darkness at the back of the cave.

No one was more attracted to the romantic possibilities of life beneath the surface of the earth than Cyrus Read Teed, a New York–born botanist who began his metaphysical researches after experiencing a divine "illumination" in the autumn of 1869. In time Dr. Teed put forth his theory that the earth is practically stationary in time and space and exists as a concave sphere, with all life on its inner surface: a gigantic inverted cave. His controversial notion was outlined in a book called *The Cellular Cosmogony, or, The Earth in a Concave Sphere,* which he wrote under his adopted name of Koresh, the Hebrew name for Cyrus. The known world is on the inside of the earth's curvature, he explained, beyond which there is only the darkness of a void. At the center of the sphere, rotating in unison, are the sun, stars, and other planets. The vast internal cavity is filled with a dense atmosphere that screens the other side of the globe.

To prove his theory, Teed measured the curvature of the earth—a measurement that contradicts the Copernican hypothesis but which has yet to be disproved. In fact he offered ten thousand dollars to anyone who could prove his theory wrong. He found plenty of takers, but each time scientific measurements were taken, the results were the same as Teed's.

Buoyed by his findings and at the same almost consumed with his passion for religion, Teed decided he needed a quiet, isolated place to work and to establish his own concept of social order. In 1894 he found such a place on the banks of the Estero River in deep southwest Florida—a 300-acre tract of land he called the Koreshan Unity, Inc. He set out to build a new society dedicated to the principles advanced in his new cosmology. Bringing about two hundred followers from Chicago, he founded his new settlement, which he named Estero, believing that the news he preached would become one of the world's great religions and that Estero would grow into a great city. He and his followers spent the next decade building houses in the wilderness. They also built a thriving tropical nursery, a handsome Art Hall, churches, tennis courts, baseball fields, marinas, a general store, and even a museum—devoted to the display and interpretation of Teed's curious teachings and scientific research. Teed eventually abandoned his medical practice altogether and proclaimed himself the messiah of a new religion called Koreshanity. He launched a newspaper, *The Flaming Sword,* which helped spread his gospel until it ceased publication in 1949.

Teed's colony never reached the population of ten million converts that had been his goal. In 1908 the old visionary died, leaving behind his unfinished colony and a personal and professional legacy steeped in legend. Among the unanswered questions are: Where did he acquire the financial resources necessary to found his colony (although his father was a successful country doctor, young Teed had to quit school to help support his large family)? How was he able to convince scores of young women—many of them married—to abandon their families and join him on his crusading pilgrimage to Florida? Who supported his scientific research?

Teed's body was placed in an immense mausoleum guarded twenty-four hours a day by teams of young women and men. In 1921, the tomb was washed away by a hurricane. In 1961 the state of Florida turned his tract of land into the Koreshan State Historic Site. Although the last of the original disciples died in 1981, site volunteers offer guided tours and slide shows of the settlement. Many of the buildings erected by the Koreshans still remain, thanks to rehabilitative and restoration efforts in recent years. Of special interest is the site's Museum and Library at the World's College of Life—Koreshan United headquarters—on Corkscrew Road along U.S. Highway 41. Here many of Teed's original books and furniture are on display, as well as an exhibit showing in three dimensions how his radical "cellular cell" theory puts the surface of the earth on the inside of the globe.

Surprises in the Sea

IN THE SPRING of 1967, the deep-diving *Aluminaut* was on a routine exploratory mission a few miles off the coast of Florida when scientists on board spotted what appeared to be an enormous highway meandering along the ocean floor three thousand feet below the surface. Intrigued, the scientists moved in for a closer inspection. The submerged "road," which appeared to be paved with manganese oxide, seemed to be part of an elaborate undersea highway system. Special wheels installed on the *Aluminaut* enabled the tiny submarine to rumble along the subterranean roadway for some distance, much as a modern automobile motors down an uncrowded interstate.

Except that this interstate was more than half a mile beneath the sea.

Subsequent voyages of exploration have thus far failed to reveal the underwater highway's origin or terminus. Assuming the phenomenon is indeed synthetic and not the result of some natural geological force as suspected by some scientists, several important questions naturally arise. Who built the colossal undersea stoneworks? When were they built, and why?

To begin our search for answers, let's go back to 1968, one year after the startling discovery off the southern coast. On a solo flight off the Florida coast, Dr. J. Manson Valentine, an American zoologist and veteran deep-sea diver, noticed what looked like a "giant wall" of stone crisscrossing the shallow

24

depths in a remarkably well-defined and geometric pattern. The structure, which was several hundred yards long and clearly visible from the air, consisted of massive stone blocks over sixteen feet square, some of which formed regular polygons, circles, triangles, rectangles, and dead straight lines extending over several miles.

Valentine, who had first noticed the formation while flying over the area ten years earlier, donned scuba gear and went down this time to investigate. He was joined by veteran French diver and engineer Dimitri Rebikoff, a pioneer of underwater photography and inventor of the Pegasus torpedo.

The two seasoned scientist-explorers were not prepared for what they saw flickering in the clear waters—the apparent remains of a long-drowned harbor, perhaps an entire city, that presumably had vanished beneath the waves countless centuries before. In the sparkling depths the duo found what may be platforms, roads, collapsed walls, and columns, some resembling the pre-Inca stonework of Peru, the pillars of Stonehenge, or the Cyclopean walls of Minoan Greece.

Carbon 14 datings of fossilized mangrove roots growing over the stones indicated the walls had been in place for at least twelve thousand years—long before the first Indians are believed to have arrived in that part of the New World. According to Valentine, the intriguing ruins consisted of

> an extensive pavement of rectangular and polygonal flat stones of varying size and thickness, obviously shaped and accurately aligned to form a convincingly artifactual arrangement. These stones had evidently laid submerged over a long span of time, for the edges of the biggest ones had become rounded off, giving the blocks the domed appearance of giant loaves of bread or pillows. Some were absolutely rectangular, sometimes approaching perfect squares.

Valentine went on to describe "avenues of apparently fitted stones, . . . mosaic-like pavements" and "three short causeways of accurately aligned large stones . . . of uniform width and that end in corner stones." From the air, Valentine said, "one can dimly make out, under their blanketing of dark algae, the huge individual stones that precisely border the margins of this geological or archaeological challenge."

Reacting to criticism from academic circles over his astounding find, Valentine said:

> My personal feeling is that this entire complex represents the intelligent utilization, by ancient man, of materials provided by nature and appropriate for the creation of some sort of ceremonial center. In this connection it should be remembered that certain ancient sacred sites, such as the Glastonbury Circle and the designs of the Nasca desert of Peru of lines and images of mile-long animals, traceable only from the air because of their gigantic proportions, have virtually no point of reference with our modern technology, as the purposes of these majestic artifacts are incomprehensible to us.

Soon after the discovery, hundreds of divers and scientists rushed to the scene, mapping, photographing, digging, and studying the ruins. Some observers considered them to be of natural origin, but many more argued that the artificial nature of the sprawling watery complex indicated it might have been constructed by an advanced civilization using superior engineering technology in remote antiquity.

For months the controversy raged. Hundreds of articles appeared in scientific journals as well as newspapers and popular magazines. Television crews from all over the world descended into the depths to probe with color cameras and stereophonic sound equipment. Rather than asking whether the ruins were synthetic, most investigators seemed more curious to know who had built the colossal structure, and when.

Predictably, archaeologists were very careful in offering opinions. Theories ranged from pre-Columbian builders—the Olmecs or possibly Mayans—to extraterrestrial connections. It was pointed out that the ruins were located in the vicinity of what has been called the Bermuda Triangle, a part of the Atlantic Ocean renowned for mysterious activity. It was inevitable that the name of Atlantis, too, would be invoked in attempting to solve the riddle of the undersea ruins. For years, searchers for the lost continent of Atlantis have looked to the warm, shallow waters between Florida and the Bahamas for clues to the sunken empire.

Most of what we know about Atlantis can be traced back to a couple of Socratic dialogues supposedly authored by Plato around 355 B.C. In *Timaeus* and *Critias,* Plato laid the basic groundwork for the theory of Atlantis, drawing upon blurry accounts handed down by questionable Egyptian priests. According to these stories, some of which were pure fairy tale, a brilliant civilization had once flowered "beyond the pillars of Hercules [thought to be the Straits of Gibraltar]," a civilization older and larger than North Africa and Asia Minor combined.

The Atlanteans, so the story went, were a "brave, handsome and virtuous" people who had achieved a high state of culture, excelling in finance, religion, the arts, and military prowess. Sometime around 12,000 B.C., however, a powerful earthquake, followed by massive volcanic eruptions and tidal waves, was said to have sunk the entire land mass in one day. Temples, palaces, fortresses, and houses toppled into the sea; overnight, millions of "proud, fair" Atlanteans were washed away, leaving only a handful of survivors who fled the devastation in swift-sailing vessels. These survivors reached the New World and either mingled with Atlanteans who had already migrated there earlier or introduced their culture into some areas for the first time.

Of the drowned "mother continent" not much more is known, yet legends of its existence persisted through the centuries. Generations of scholars since Plato have been unable to establish whether the story of Atlantis was a product of the philosopher's imagination or whether he was deliberately misinformed by his sources. Even skeptics do not rule out the possibility that the story of Atlantis might have been based on historical fact, but they stop short of embracing the idea due mainly to outrageous claims about the continent's antiquity.

Since the dawn of recorded history, the memory of disastrous floods has haunted the human consciousness, beginning perhaps with Noah's biblical account of the Great Flood. That episode was probably based on an even earlier Mesopotamian story told in the Gilgamesh epic, which might itself have been formed from yet a much older legend. In the New World, Indians living along the southern coast and eastern flanks of the Appalachians believed their ancestors had come from across the great sea. Farther south, the ancient Aztecs told the Spanish conquistadores that their grandfathers—the people of Az—had come from Aztlan, a sunken land in the east, and that the "fair god" Quetzalcoatl, a white-bearded teacher, had also come from a land "beyond the swelling waves." Could Aztlan have been ancient Atlantis? Is it possible that survivors from a catastrophic upheaval somewhere far out in the Atlantic made their way across the angry waves to the nearest safe ground— a refuge that would later be called the United States? Some scholars theorize that these scattered survivors who reached the southern coast of the New World settled along the coast of the Carolinas, Georgia, Florida, Mexico, Central and South America, and the islands of the Caribbean.

After marrying into local Indian tribes, these "superior" foreigners helped engineer the construction of dazzling cities of stone and colossal highways spanning Yucatan, some of which now lie buried and forgotten beneath the waves.

Supporters of the Atlantis theory point out that less than a century ago the cities of Troy and Mycenae were considered myths as well. Their discovery and subsequent excavation by the self-taught German scholar Heinrich Schliemann (1822-1890) has become a model for many champions of the Atlantis theme. In the words of Prince Michael of Greece: "The rehabilitation of Homer and the belated but definitive victory of those who believed him may give food for thought to those who doubt the existence of Atlantis."

To add to the lingering mystery of Atlantis, Edgar Cayce, the famous "sleeping prophet" of Virginia Beach, Virginia, in

1945 predicted that "in 1968 or 1969" a portion of Atlantis would rise from the sea off the Coast of Florida.

Cayce, considered one of the world's greatest clairvoyants until his death in 1946, claimed Atlantis was situated somewhere between the Gulf of Mexico and the Straits of Gibraltar. His colorful and detailed descriptions of the vanished continent, which came while the prophet was said to be in a deep trance, bear a remarkable resemblance to the southern United States as it is in the last quarter of the twentieth century.

Cayce himself, who professed to know little about history and even less about ancient civilizations, was surprised at his own repeated references to Atlantis. Commenting on one statement attributed to him during a hypnotic sleep, Cayce said:"I wonder where that came from and if there is anything to it?" In 1933 he predicted that "a portion of the temple [of Atlantis] may yet be discovered under the slime of ages of sea water—near what is known as Bimini, off the coast of Florida."

Seven years later his prediction was more precise: "And Poseidia [Atlantis] will be among the first portions of Atlantis to rise again. Expect it in 'sixty-eight or 'sixty-nine. Not so far away!"

When the underwater structure off the Florida coast was discovered in 1968—exactly as foretold by Cayce—waves of joy and satisfaction rippled through Cayce's followers. Vindication had never been sweeter for these die-hard devotees of the Virginia psychic, objects of considerable ridicule and scorn by the established scientific community. Their leader had been right all along, so they believed, and now the restless ocean was spitting up the evidence to prove it—just as Cayce had foretold.

Atlantologists and Cayce followers pointed to the stunning architectural features now emerging from the depths—eroded marble and stone columns, some with tongue-and-groove edges, traces of finely tempered color, and long rows of brood-' ing stone blocks that could have only been chiseled and laid in place by refined engineering techniques. The subterranean finds, including the mysterious roadway off the southern coast, fired the imagination of Atlantologists around the world.

Shortly after the discovery, a group of English newspapermen voted the reemergence of Atlantis as the "fourth most important news story they could imagine—five places ahead of the Second Coming of Christ."

It was a remarkable time for believers in Atlantis. Textbooks would have to be rewritten to include whole chapters on the once-fabled civilization, now rising slowly from the depths of the ocean. Television documentaries were being released by the dozen; magazine and newspaper articles brimmed with illustrated references to the sunken continent. An entire generation was in the grip of "Atlantis fever" as new finds were brought forth from the deep.

In academic circles, however, the ivory towers remained drawn up tight, stoically warding off the flurry of unsubstantiated claims being hurled at them from advocates of Atlantis. At best, the established community said, Atlantis was only one of several possible romantic explanations for the existence of these peculiar undersea ruins.

"Official" theories as to the origin and nature of the stone walls ranged from Indian fish traps to underwater storage pens for conch shells, sponges, or turtles. One archaeologist suspected the stone walls were laid by local Carib Indians, even though it seems fairly certain that at the time of the discovery of America this tribe did not build in stone. Others have attributed the subterranean construction to Spanish explorers, calling it a "blockhouse" without revealing why it happens to be underwater.

The lack of records, oral or written, means that we probably will have to wait until more conclusive research is conducted before knowing for sure whether the undersea megaplex off the southern coast is some kind of weird but natural geological formation or the remains of a brilliant civilization that vanished thousands of years ago.

Voyagers
From Beyond

In Search of Cofitachequi

ALONG THE BANKS of the Savannah River in what is now South Carolina there once lived a people of uncommon grace and elegance. Their kingdom, known as Cofitachequi, or "Dog Town," consisted of several small villages and communities, most of which were constructed around a series of handsome, pyramid-shaped earthen mounds. Unlike most of their neighbors on each side of the winding river, the people of Cofitachequi were a peaceful lot, preferring to settle disputes by arbitration than with spears and tomahawks. They were ruled by a young queen whose stunning features and regal countenance were later compared to another great female leader, Cleopatra of ancient Egypt. The woods along the river fairly bristled with game, and the gentle climate was ideally suited for growing a variety of crops—including corn, squash, and golden stalks of tobacco. It was in many ways a paradise for the thousand or so Indians who called Cofitachequi home.

In the summer of 1540, no one had reason to think it would ever end. But a few hundred miles to the south, near what is now Tampa Bay, Florida, several "strange houses" that floated on water had been seen unloading more foreigners and their terrifying animals on four legs. The white-skinned strangers were said to be clad in shiny "skin" that burned like the sun, and they carried noisy sticks that made smoke and fire at will.

Still, in spite of such alarming reports, the gentle people of Cofitachequi had no reason to fear the far-off arrival of such outsiders. Life went on as before. The men fished and hunted;

the women cooked and tended the fields.

But the man called Captain Don Hernando De Soto would change all that soon. Already, as his gold-hungry conquistadores trudged north through the swamps of northern Florida, the tall, bearded Spaniard was dreaming of the fabled treasures that he knew awaited him at Cofitachequi.

Gold! The very sound of the word was enough to make De Soto's eyes light up. He trembled as he recalled the mounds of precious stones he had seized from the people of Peru only a few years earlier. Enough gold to fill up several rooms! Now he was about to add to his fabulous personal fortune. And it all seemed so easy. What was there to prevent him and his battle-hardened soldiers—six hundred strong of Spain's finest infantry, cavalry, and scouts—from taking what they wanted in this raw, untamed new world? Certainly not a few naked savages armed with spears and knives!

By any standard, De Soto was already rich. Most of his wealth had been attained during his participation in the bloody conquest of the Inca Empire in Peru. Not only had he been appointed governor of Cuba, he owned a handsome villa in Havana and several pieces of valuable property back in Spain.

But he was unhappy. He wanted more, lots more. His biggest dream now was finding Eldorado, the legendary city of gold which he believed to be somewhere beyond Florida, hidden in vast, wild regions that would later be known as Georgia and South Carolina.

Others had said the city lay in the deserts of the great Southwest. Rumors circulating in Madrid and Havana placed it first in Mexico, then Colorado, Arizona, and New Mexico. De Soto, however, had reason to believe Eldorado lay somewhere in the southeastern part of what was to become the United States of America.

On May 18, 1539, he and his hand-picked army had set sail in a large fleet for the northlands. A few days later they landed near Tampa Bay and immediately set off in search of the city of gold. Besides his soldiers, the retinue included twelve priests, four friars, two secretaries, servants, cattle, horses, mules, thirteen sows, and several boars—the first hogs to be seen on the American continent. De Soto also traveled with a pack of Irish bloodhounds. Whenever captured Indians wouldn't cooperate, he had them thrown to the vicious dogs for sport.

Before reaching Georgia, De Soto's army passed through Apalachee, near what is now Tallahassee, where they demanded to know from the local population the whereabouts of the lost city of gold. Whenever their questions went unanswered, the Spaniards would summarily execute Indians at random, enslave a few others, then burn down the village. On at least one occasion, the captain ordered a captured Indian to be burned alive for refusing to talk.

Finally, stories began to come forth from terrified villagers about the place De Soto was seeking. At swordpoint, these Indians were only too happy to describe a glittering city just beyond the forest, or just over the next ridge, a city said to be filled with the stones of gold he was searching for. Some even offered to show him the way—anything to rid their village of his cruel presence. More often than not, once the Spanish army was safely out of town, their volunteer guides would pretend to be so sick they couldn't go any farther. Some simply fled into the woods to escape.

Whenever they heard he was coming, some Indians would abandon their villages, preferring to let the fire-brandishing foreigner march through rather than risk confrontation. After the army had left, the villagers would safely return to what remained of their community.

Once the Spaniards reached southwestern Georgia, travel became extremely difficult. The forests were dark and thick and many of the rivers impassable. To make matters worse, hostile Indians constantly harassed the arrogant band of outsiders, shooting venom-tipped arrows at them whenever the opportunity arose.

Still the Europeans pressed on through the wilderness, guided by scouts who frequently took the wrong trail or deliberately misled them in other ways. The patience of the conquistadore was beginning to wear thin. Many of his men began to urge him to halt the expedition, to turn around now and go back home.

But they had come too far to go back home empty-handed. Surely, thought the commander, the city of gold was near. He could almost smell the glittering substance.

Finally, on May Day, 1540, Hernando De Soto and his weary, hungry, and footsore men stumbled from a dense pine thicket into a clearing along the Rio Dulce (Savannah River), just south of present-day Augusta, Georgia. Immediately they were greeted by four canoes carrying several young men and women. In one of the canoes rode the queen of Cofitachequi herself.

After formally welcoming the strangers with wreaths of flowers and strings of pearls, the "Lady of Cofitachequi" invited them into her city to eat and rest. On the way into town, the conquistadore was beside himself with joy. At last he had reached his Eldorado, the lost city of gold! But here it was known as Cofitachequi.

Rudely, De Soto began looking around for signs of the treasure. He ordered his men to search every hut and every mound in the village, to question every Indian—man, woman and child—about gold.

One is tempted to try to imagine what must have been going on inside the captain's mind that day. Visions of gold-bedecked villagers, such as those he had encountered with Pizarro in Peru so long before, must have filled his head. He probably remembered the jewel-encrusted tombs, the temples and government buildings laden with precious stones. Here, in this quaint little kingdom on the wild American frontier, he no doubt expected to find similar treasures.

Alas, not a single precious stone was to be found anywhere. There were no necklaces or rings of gold, no silver ornaments or ruby adornments. In fact, the Indians of Cofitachequi had never even heard of gold! The only valuables they had to offer were pieces of copper and mica and some glittering strands of freshwater pearls.

After a few uneventful days in Cofitachequi, De Soto had had enough. Accepting fresh supplies from the generous queen—tanned skins, blankets, strips of venison, dry wafers, and a large quantity of "very good salt"—he decided to push on, but not before first stripping the village of every strand of pearl in sight. Methodically his men went from house to house and temple to temple snatching anything they considered of value. Soon their pockets and satchels were bulging with shiny, round pearls, so many they didn't bother to collect those that spilled out onto the ground.

When the queen saw that the only way to spare her village from the torch lay in her cunning, she led the Spaniards to another town within her kingdom called Talomico, said to be a special religious center, where she allowed them to plunder a large temple mound decorated inside and out with strings of finely polished pearls.

Still not satisfied, and disheartened at his failure to find gold, De Soto resorted to one last dastardly act. When the queen told him—presumably in a desperate final attempt to rid her people of the Spanish scourge—that the golden metal he was looking for lay in another province a few days' journey from Cofitachequi, De Soto insisted she come along as a guide.

This action understandably angered the natives, but they were powerless to do anything but watch their beloved queen hauled away in chains before the marauding band of soldiers. A few miles downstream, however, she managed to escape, along with a couple of servants who had volunteered to accompany her on the forced march.

The Lady of Cofitachequi eventually made her way safely back home, but the tiny, once-tranquil kingdom would never be the same again. Besides looting their villages, the Spaniards had also infected the Indians with a plague-like disease, and soon the riverside empire of Cofitachequi disappeared, along with its legends of gold.

Do Soto continued marching north into North Carolina, eventually crossing the Blue Ridge Mountains into Cherokee territory, then beyond into Alabama, Mississippi, and Louisiana. But he never found his lost city of gold.

In May of 1542, almost two years to the day after plundering Cofitachequi, De Soto died, presumably from a fever contracted along the Mississippi River. Chroniclers of his adventures say he never got over his failure to find gold in Cofitachequi and died a broken man.

On the Trail of Prince Madoc

MANY STRANGE STORIES have been advanced to account for the origin and development of native American cultures. Some legends tell how fleeing survivors from the sinking continent of Atlantis made their way across the sea to settle in the wilds of the New World, where they spawned a new race of reddish-colored people. Others claim that centuries ago shipwrecked sailors from Iberia or Gaul somehow mingled with Indians already living along the southern coast to produce a noble stock of blue-eyed savages. Still other theories hold that it was the ancient Egyptians or Libyans who somehow survived perilous voyages across the ocean either to become the first Americans or at least to influence inhabitants already here. For years many scholars believed the Israelites might have landed on the North American continent, presumably in southern waters, where they intermarried with local tribes and eventually transferred aspects of their culture.

To defend their theories, scholars often point to striking similarities in languages, customs, dress, habits, and other cultural traits between native Americans and whatever group of oceangoing voyagers they happened to be favoring at any given point. In the eighteenth century, for example, a British trader named James Adair claimed he heard chanting Choctaw and Chickasaw Indians use the word "Jehovah" and other Jewish terms which suggested to him that the Indians were descended from the Ten Lost Tribes of Israel.

Adair's astounding claim was only one of many such tales

coming to light as European explorers and settlers pushed deeper into the southern hinterlands. Contact with the local inhabitants, whether friendly or hostile, always evoked the same question: Who were these red-skinned people and where had they come from?

Since there was no mention of them in the Bible, invading Europeans eventually declared them to be subhuman. Some even thought they were devils, outcasts after the Fall of humanity. And since such was the case, it seemed appropriate that they should be dealt with accordingly by superior, God-fearing Christian colonizers and conquistadores. That is, nobody—especially these half-naked, red-skinned savages—had any moral, religious, or legal right to stand in their way. And as soon as gold was discovered in the hills of southern Appalachia, this determination took on new meaning.

It was just such an attitude, which seemed to grow coarser with time, that helped to justify the Europeans' ruthless exploitation of the local inhabitants of the North American continent, as well as lands to the south. Besides, there was a war going on, an undeclared war to control territory and commercial enterprises in the New World. Anyone who interfered—and there was special reference to native Americans—had to be shoved aside to make way for expansion and development. Even when the Church officially recognized the unfortunate natives as humans after all, it still didn't alter the official policies of conquest, conversion, and extermination set into motion by the Spanish and continued by the French and English. Europeans arriving in North America still didn't know what to make of the strange, secretive, occasionally docile population they encountered.

As European exploration went on, stories began to crop up about a mysterious race of white-skinned Indians that lived just beyond some craggy ridge or forest. Crouched around a campfire late at night in the wilds of this strange new land, settlers found it easy to fantasize about the existence of such curious beings. If these "white" Indians existed, then the conclusion was obvious: at some time in the remote past, other European travelers had to have reached these lonely shores. If so, it was only natural that they would have inter-mingled with host tribes, either as masters or as captives.

From these modest beginnings, one of America's most enduring myths was born—that of a superior "white" race of Indian that supposedly ruled over portions of the New World long before Christopher Columbus's epic-making voyage in 1492. Even today, stories of blond, blue-eyed Indians live on in the folklore of the southeastern United States.

The search for white Indians began in earnest in 1666 after Morgan Jones, chaplain to the governor of Virginia, narrowly escaped death at the hands of a fierce tribe of "British-speaking" Indians while on an expedition in the Carolinas. Jones, a Welshman, said the group of Tuscarora Indians spoke in a tongue that sounded similar to that of his ancestral home-land. The Indians spared his life when they discovered they shared the same language.

Within a few years, fair-skinned Indians, many of whom were said to be fluent in Welsh, were discovered elsewhere in the Carolinas, Virginia, Kentucky, Tennessee, Georgia, Alabama, Florida, and other nearby regions. Daniel Boone himself told of coming upon a band of "blue-eyed" Indians who he thought spoke with a British dialect, probably Welsh, "though I have no means of assessing their language."

Perhaps the most popular "white Indian" tale of all centered around the mythological adventures of a young Welsh prince named Madoc, or Modoc, whose full name was Madoc ab Owain Gwynedd of Wales. According to several accounts, no doubt embellished over the centuries, Madoc led a convoy of settlers to the New World in 1170, arriving in Mobile Bay, Alabama, before fanning out with about 120 followers on expeditions that traversed several states in the Southeast.

No one is sure what brought the legendary Welsh prince to America in the first place. It is true that a bloody civil war was raging in his homeland at the time. Many Welsh families emigrated to escape the bloodshed, with most settling else-where in Britain and on the continent. There is no reason to doubt that Madoc, fleeing the turmoil for the same reasons, could have been blown off course, eventually landing in

America as legend purports.

It is also reasonable to assume that the prince would have had the nautical skills, and perhaps even the inspiration, to embark on a trans-oceanic voyage of such a magnitude. Though not exactly common, tales of a vast, uncharted land far to the west were being circulated among Welsh seamen and explorers as early as the twelfth century. Many of these stories, no doubt, had their origins in ancient Viking sagas.

According to historian Humphrey Lhoyd's *Historie of Cambria*, written in 1584, Prince Madoc not only discovered North America, but also returned home to round up "more of his own nation, acquaintance, and freends to inhabit that fayre and large countrie, [and] went thither again." The first voyage reportedly took the settlers as far as Mobile Bay, Alabama, where he immediately set out to explore lands to the west in Mississippi, Louisiana, Arkansas, and Texas, and as far east and north as North Carolina and Georgia.

Lhoyd claims that after the war in Wales had ended Madoc returned home and reported having found a fruitful land to the west where he had left some of his people. Then he collected ten more shiploads of colonists and went away for good. One version puts the number of ships at eighteen and the number of colonists at more than three thousand.

Later, when Spanish conquistadores captured Mexico, they learned from Montezuma that the imperial Aztec leader was descended from a mysterious race of fair-skinned people that had come "from a generation very far away, in a little island in the north." Wales, perhaps? What sounds incredible might not be so farfetched when one considers the research of Dr. Barry Fell, formerly a professor at Harvard University. In his book *America, B.C.*, Fell draws on hard evidence to support his theory that North America was visited not once but numerous times in prehistory by several groups of Old World sea voyagers, including Egyptians, Phoenicians, Iberians, Libyans, and perhaps even the Israelites. To defend his thesis, Fell points beyond the archaeological record alone to architectural, linguistic, religious, and other cultural similarities between American Indian groups and those of some ancient peoples.

41

For more than a century, archaeologists have indeed puzzled over the origin of several unexplained stone forts and buildings scattered throughout highland areas of the southeastern United States, particularly in Georgia, Tennessee, and Alabama. Old Stone Fort, near Chattanooga, Tennessee, for example, resembles a medieval castle—a Welsh castle, complete with walls and a single gateway and moat fed by the Duck River. The remains of Old Stone Fort, Fort Mountain, near Chatsworth, Georgia, and De Soto Falls in Alabama have intrigued visitors and scholars for years with their strange, zigzagging pattern of construction, isolated locations, and other traits that hint of pre-Columbian origin.

At Fort Mountain, bronze markers along the trail leading up to the fort make vague reference to the mysterious "moon-eyed" white people mentioned in Cherokee legend. They also mention other fanciful visitors to the area, including the legendary Prince Madoc, whose name has been linked to several other stone markings and petroglyphs in other parts of the Southeast.

Fort Mountain's 855-foot wall, which weaves back and forth along the rock crest of the mountain like a gigantic, petrified serpent, averages two to three feet in height and up to twelve feet in width. Archaeologists speculate that the circular wall might have been higher at one time—perhaps as high as seven feet. And this, many contend, rules out the possibility that local Indians themselves might have built the wall. Why? Simply because they lacked the tools or engineering technology necessary for erecting such impressive monuments and structures at that time in prehistory!

Unfortunately, there are few of these ancient stoneworks around to help shed light on pre-Columbian contacts with the New World. As a result, scientists often turn to the oral record left behind by the Amerinds themselves.

In his book *The Secret*, archaeologist Joe Mahan points to convincing evidence that the forebears of native Americans were radically influenced by contacts with ancient European voyagers. This evidence, handed down by the Yuchi Indians of the southeastern United States, strongly suggests that certain tribes—principally the Cherokees, Chickasaws, and Creeks—were descended from the "lost" Ten Tribes of Israel. Mahan also suspects that the Yuchi are a much older group of Indians than originally believed. He urges other scholars to step up studies of this remarkable group of people in order to better understand their dramatic legends and myths that link them with Old World cultures.

What are we to make of these old legends? Is it possible that "white-skinned gods" walked among the Indians of North American many thousands of years before Columbus's landing in 1492? Were these "gods" actually the shipwrecked survivors of ancient sailing vessels from Europe, Asia, or Africa, perhaps lost or blown off course? Did these survivors intermingle with the natives, influencing their cultural development over the centuries, as suggested by the likes of Adair, Fell, and Mahan? Or are these ancient trans-Atlantic voyages mere myth, myths spawned and perpetrated by self-serving Europeans who saw in them the ethnocentric ammunition needed to enslave a race of people, thereby aiding in their exploitation of the New World?

Some have carved their answers to many of these questions onto a bronze memorial tablet in Mobile Bay, Alabama. The tablet, erected in 1953, reads: "In memory of Prince Madoc, a Welsh explorer, who landed on the shores of Mobile Bay in 1170 and left behind, with the Indians, the Welsh language."

The Restless Skies

IT WAS A night of inky calm, a perfect night for flying. George Smith, a 22-year-old commercial aviator from Quitman, Georgia, a small town in the southwest corner of the state, had just finished dusting a tobacco field in a nearby county and was heading home. Five miles from the airport he happened to glance out his rear window. That's when he saw it—a bright, cigar-shaped light hovering over an isolated patch of woods.

"It was the most incredible thing I'd ever seen in my life," the young pilot later told a local reporter. "It just hung there over the trees, flashing like some kind of lit-up Christmas ornament."

The next day a farmer riding his tractor near Albany "nearly had a heart attack" when a shiny, round object the size of a motorhome whooshed by overhead. That afternoon two state patrolmen near Lakeland, Georgia, watched a mysterious object float slowly over the courthouse for about five minutes, then vanish in a puff of smoke.

In the days and weeks that followed, hundreds of such sightings were reported throughout Georgia, from the mountains in the north to the heavily populated coastal shores. Meanwhile, hundreds of other reports of unidentified flying objects (UFOs) were jamming telephone lines at police stations and military bases from Jacksonville, Florida, to Jackson, Mississippi.

That summer of 1974 was one of the busiest on record for UFO watchers in the South. Thousands of unexplained aerial phenomena were reported across vast areas of the region, primarily in Georgia, Florida, Alabama, Mississippi, and the Carolinas. Eyewitnesses included policemen, firemen, farmers, politicians, students, commercial and military pilots and at least one governor—Jimmy Carter of Georgia. The wave of sightings made front page news throughout the summer, as an aroused populace craned their heads skyward night after night in hopes of catching a glimpse of an extraterrestrial airship.

Although they are considered modern, unidentified flying objects are really nothing new. Sightings of strange objects dashing, darting, and dancing through the skies were reported in ancient times, beginning with the Egyptians and Babylonians. One of the first written accounts of a close encounter with what sounds like extraterrestrials, recorded on a 3,000-year-old papyrus scroll, is found in the annals of Thutmose III, who reigned over Egypt around 1504 B.C.

> In the year 22, of the 3rd month of winter, sixth hour of the day . . . the scribes of the House of Life found it was a circle of fire that was coming in the sky. . . . It had no head, the breath of its mouth had a foul odor. Its body was one rod long and one rod wide. It had no voice. Their hearts became confused through it; then they laid themselves on their bellies. . . .

The article goes on to describe how the scribes rushed to the Pharaoh to report the strange sight in the heavens, whereupon

> His Majesty ordered . . . an examination of all which is written in the papyrus rolls of the House of Life. His Majesty was meditating upon what happened. Now after some days had passed, these things became more numerous in the skies than ever. They shone more in the sky than the brightness of the sun, and extended to the limits of the four supports of the heavens.

In the Bible, numerous references are made to "flaming

45

chariots" and "burning lights" in the sky. Perhaps the most famous of all such sightings is found in the Book of Ezekiel, in which the prophet describes what clearly sounds like some kind of spaceship descending near the Chebar River in Chaldea around 592 B.C.: "As I looked, behold, a stormy wind came out of the north, and a great cloud, with brightness round about it, and fire flashing forth continually, and in the midst of the fire, as if it were gleaming bronze." The star-struck prophet continues to describe how "four living creatures" emerged from the strange craft, creatures who

> had the form of men, but each had four faces, and each of them had four wings. Their legs were straight, and the soles of their feet were like the sole of a calf's foot; and they sparkled like burnished bronze.
>
> Under their wings on their four sides they had human hands . . . Each had the face of a man in front: the four had the face of a lion on the right side, . . . the face of an ox on the left side, and . . . the face of an eagle at the back. . . . And their wings were spread out above; each creature had two wings, each of which touched the wing of another, while two covered their bodies.
>
> And each [creature] went straight forward . . . without turning as they went. . . . And the living creatures darted to and fro, like a flashing of lightning.

For centuries scholars have debated who—or what—the humanoid occupants of Ezekiel's vision might have been. Were they indeed angels descending from heaven, as the aged prophet believed? Or were they astronauts from outer space, clad in gleaming space-suits and brandishing unknown weapons?

The Swiss writer Erich von Daniken has become a millionaire selling books proclaiming that Ezekiel's visitors were indeed visitors from beyond the stars, returning to earth on one of their regular missions for reasons not yet clear. Other writers have compared the prophet's vision to countless other stories of aerial phenomena down through the ages and have come to the somewhat startling conclusion that these "living creatures" were actually stellar beings, sent to earth to help humanity along the road to civilization.

Ezekiel's disturbing account continues:

> Now as I looked at the living creatures, I saw a wheel upon the earth beside the living creatures, one for each of the four of them. As for the appearance of the wheels and their construction: their appearance was like the gleaming of a chrysolite . . . being as it were a wheel within a wheel. . . . The four wheels had rims and they had spokes; and their rims were full of eyes round about. And when the living creatures went, the wheels went with them; and when the living creatures rose from the earth, the wheels rose.

Throughout the 1800s, hundreds of reports of strange flying lights and cigar or barrel-shaped "airships" appeared in European, American, and Canadian periodicals. "Ghost rockets" were spotted over the northern regions of Europe in 1946. These unexplained airborne objects resembled "glowing vapors spewing a tail of smoke."

Norwegian airline pilots radioed control stations that they had observed "luminous missiles" emitting bluish-green flames and flying at speeds in excess of 6,700 miles per hour at altitudes ranging from 25,000 feet down to the level of tree-tops.

But the modern age of flying saucers actually began on June 24, 1947, when Kenneth Arnold, a civilian pilot from Boise, Idaho, saw nine gleaming objects streaking through the sky at an astonishing velocity of 1,600 miles per hour, nearly three times the capability of aircraft in those days. Arnold's detailed description of the aircraft—"flat like a pie pan and so shiny they reflected the sun like a mirror . . . flying like a saucer would if you skipped it across water"—gave rise to a new phrase in the English dictionary: flying saucer.

The years following the Korean War saw a surge in flying saucer sightings, from China to the Carolinas. The U.S. Air

Force was eventually prompted to form a special department whose sole purpose was to investigate and evaluate UFO reports. After thousands of case studies, however, Project Blue Book finally concluded in 1969 that UFOs posed no threat to national security and that there "was no evidence the sighted objects were of extraterrestrial origin." The government project was then terminated and all its files declassified.

That did not mean the end of UFO sightings. On the contrary, that same year—1969—the governor of Georgia stood on the doorsteps of a building in Leary, Georgia, watching what he and other eyewitnesses believed was a formation of unidentified flying objects streaking by overhead. About a dozen people were in the company of the governor at the time; all agreed they had definitely seen something mysterious.

In a newspaper article, Carter was quoted as saying: "I am convinced that UFOs exist because I've seen one. . . . It was a very peculiar aberration, but about twenty people saw it. . . . It was the darndest thing I've ever seen. It was big; it was very bright; it changed colors; and it was about the size of the moon. We watched it for ten minutes, but none of us could figure out what it was."

Four years later Carter filled out a detailed report form for the National Investigation Committee on Aerial Phenomena (NICAP) in which he described the object as having been erratic in flight, about 30 degrees above the horizon, and perhaps 300 to 1,000 yards distant.

A few months after Carter filed the NICAP report, the wave of UFO sightings in the South was on. Television stations, newspapers, and magazines carried daily stories on the sightings, while wire services broadcast the reports around the world. It was a time of terrific national and international tension. Watergate and Vietnam were still on the minds of most Americans, and the Soviet Union and United States had entered a new phase of the escalating arms race. Long gasoline lines at service stations and reduced speed limits were right around the corner.

People who study the UFO phenomenon theorize that most waves of sightings coincide with troubled times—wars, economic depressions, domestic turmoil. Others see a relationship between military buildups—especially of nuclear forces—and the frequency of reports of UFOs. The idea seems to be that extraterrestrial explorers orbiting the earth hail from civilizations far more advanced than ours and therefore possess the wisdom necessary to guide us through dangerous times.

In 1952, for example, at the height of the Korean War, dozens of UFO sightings were reported over Asia near the site of the conflict. But one close encounter in Florida that year was the first episode where a UFO left tangible evidence. It involved three Boy Scouts, their scoutmaster, and a lonely Florida road at night.

C.S. Desverges was driving the young scouts home from a camping trip when, about 9:00 p.m., on the night of August 19, 1952, he spotted a strange light hovering over a palmetto thicket just off the road. Desverges stopped the car, instructed the boys to run for help if he wasn't back in fifteen minutes, then set off to investigate. He carried only a flashlight and a machete, which he used to hack his way through the dense underbrush.

The scoutmaster wasn't prepared for the sight that awaited him in the woods. A large, flat object seemed to be hovering about thirty to forty feet above ground, supported by thin, metallic legs protruding to the ground. At that point he noticed a sudden rise in temperature and detected a foul odor. As he advanced toward the curious object, the heat became almost unbearable.

A few yards away, Desverges was able to make out the object's shape and density—large and disk-shaped, he later recalled, and its underpart concave. He noticed also a dome over the center of the strange craft, which he made out to be smooth and gray in color.

Suddenly he heard a sound "like the opening of a well-oiled door," and a tiny red ball that grew into a red, misty cloud drifted toward him. The instant the mist engulfed him, he fainted.

The scouts, meanwhile, had watched their leader march

deeper into the dark woods, following the sweep of light from his flashlight. Unable to see the large object occupying so much of Desverges's attention, they were startled when a bright red light exploded over the spot where they thought the scoutmaster might be. Frightened, the boys scrambled out of the car and raced to a nearby farmhouse for help.

Desverges had recovered by the time the sheriff's deputies arrived, but was found stumbling along the road, talking incoherently. As soon as his orientation returned, he led the officers to the spot in the woods where the strange red light had overcome him. Other than his flashlight—and a few flattened weeds—they found nothing out of the ordinary. On the drive back to town, however, Desverges noticed that the hair on his arms and hands had been singed. He also found slight burns on his arms.

An official investigation was conducted over the next few days, but whatever Desverges encountered that August night in 1952 remains a mystery.

The Colony of Rugby

ONCE UPON A time, on a high mountaintop in eastern Tennessee, there occurred one of the strangest colonization movements in American history. While wagon trains rolled westward and gunfighters shot it out in places like Dodge City and Tombstone, a group of English aristocrats, accompanied by lords, ladies, dukes, and representatives of the queen, moved into this rugged high country wilderness to carve out a new life. Instead of guns, plows, mules, and axes, they brought with them soccer balls, pianos, books, and banquet tables.

The unusual group of settlers, which began arriving in the late 1870s, was part of a bold new social experiment launched by Thomas Hughes, a nineteenth-century British author and social reformer. The colony, called Rugby, was Hughes's attempt to put together a new society in the American wilderness based on the utopian ideals of his time. In the decade that Hughes's community flourished, it was a cultural showplace. Famous artists, poets, writers, philosophers, and scientists from all over the world flocked to Rugby to participate in what Hughes proclaimed as the "new Jerusalem."

A prominent member of Parliament, judge, and queen's counselor, Hughes was also the popular author of *Tom Brown's Schooldays,* in which he criticized contemporary British society. His writings eventually helped bring about widespread changes in England's child labor practices and corrupt educational system. Hughes was also a spokesman for the Christian Socialists and founded the Working Men's College. At age

51

sixty-two he founded Rugby, his utopian dream in the New World, the experiment he referred to as "my last castle in Spain." This dream was spawned at least in part by his concern for the plight of the younger sons of British aristocracy, victims of primogeniture, the social system in which all inherited estates went exclusively to the oldest son. Since manual labor was considered beneath them, the young squires had no choice but to enter already overcrowded professional fields or "starve like gentlemen." Many who followed Hughes to America were younger sons of wealthy families, who preferred to start anew in the wilderness rather than suffer the indignity of having to seek work at home. Others, perhaps, were bored with daily life as members of the privileged upper class in Victorian England, and were lured across the Atlantic by the call of the wild.

Hughes later wrote: "We are able to open a town here, a new center of human life, human interests, human activities . . . in this strangely beautiful solitude; a center in which a healthy, hopeful, reverent life shall grow." His plan was to establish a self-sustaining community in which people would carve their own estates out of the wilderness and still enjoy the "good life" associated with British learning and culture.

The community was founded atop a steep plateau surrounded by virgin timberlands and rushing river gorges, about seventy miles northwest of modern-day Knoxville. Originally named Plateau, the colony was renamed Rugby after Hughes's alma mater, Rugby School in England, and was dedicated on October 5, 1880. Its growth followed a sophisticated town plan that emphasized aesthetic rather than practical considerations. Eventually about seventy buildings graced the trim, well-manicured townscape, many with the high peaked roofs, gabled windows, and decorative millwork typical of the Victorian era. A tastefully designed and furnished hotel was built—the Tabard Inn, named after the inn in Chaucer's *Canterbury Tales.* A public library, with thousands of volumes donated by publishers and other admirers, was the pride of the colony. Tea houses were also planned, of course, as well as tennis lawns, theaters, elegant restaurants, and hotels with impeccable accommodations. Fancy clothing shops would follow, as would other trappings of a civilized society.

Elaborate gardens also abounded in Rugby. Park land was set aside for common use. Trails were built into surrounding river gorges. Lawn tennis grounds were established. Highways were laid out and given English names—Donnington, Farringdon, Reading, Longcott. The town also published its own newspaper, *The Rugbeian*, which was widely read throughout Europe and America.

Rugby quickly gained international attention, arousing curiosity among people who followed its progress through every crisis and triumph. Travel to the colony became fashionable as steamship lines devised and advertised excursions to Rugby from Liverpool, England, via Philadelphia and Cincinnati. Arriving visitors prepared to face a harsh environment were pleasantly surprised to discover just how much the wilderness had been transformed into a little "new England." There were riding and hunt clubs, comfortable country clubs, and teas galore. Literary and drama clubs had sprung up, as did a tennis team that competed against champions from England and elsewhere in the United States.

While other Tennesseeans snickered at their fancy new neighbors, the British colonists went about their carefree ways unruffled, day after day, year after year, season after season. They ate, drank, and played excessively, mimicking their contemporary counterparts back home. Just because they had chosen to live in the wilderness did not mean they had to give up the good life. So Rugby flourished for a decade, reaching a peak population in 1884 of 450.

But its early years were marked by adversity as well—severe winters, droughts, and, during the long summer of 1881, a typhoid epidemic that took several lives. Some townsfolk attempted to establish a tomato canning factory and a pottery business, neither of which succeeded. Efforts to raise livestock, grain, fruit, and vegetables met similar fates. From the beginning, the Rugby colonists were beset with problems, many stemming from the fact they would rather play than work. Priority was placed on cultural and recreational activities. Attending afternoon teas and tennis matches was preferable to plowing cornfields and mending fences. Fancy-dress balls were common, as was participation in social, musical, dramatic, tennis, soccer, and baseball clubs.

By 1887, the year of Queen Victoria's Jubilee Celebration, the colony had entered its twilight. *The Rugbeian* had ceased publication, several buildings had burned or collapsed, and settlers were leaving the colony for England or resettlement in the United States.

In spite of Rugby's numerous problems, however, Hughes cherished hopes for his colony's success to the end of his life. In 1896, in a letter to some Rugby friends, he wrote, "I may not see Rugby again. . . . I can't help feeling and believing that good seed was sown when Rugby was founded, and that someday the reapers . . . will come along with joy bearing heavy sheaves with them."

After the turn of the century, with most of the original colonists gone, Rugby settled into a small farming community of about 125 residents. Today the town has only about 70 inhabitants, some of whom are descended from the original colonists.

Seventeen of the original buildings still stand, and most of them open their doors to the public each July during the town's annual pilgrimage celebration. Visitors can stroll through the town's historic buildings, including Christ Church, Episcopal—with its original hanging lamps and 1849 rosewood reed organ, believed to be the oldest in the United States; the Thomas Hughes Public Library, unchanged since its doors opened in 1882; and Kingstone Lisle, the resort home built for Hughes. The library, containing seven thousand rare books, is considered one of the finest collections of Victorian literature in the New World.

Caves, Comets, And Killer Storms

Last Island's Last Day

ON THE MORNING of August 9, 1856, early risers along the Louisiana coast marveled at a magnificent, copper-colored dawn breaking over the Gulf of Mexico. A few were reminded of the old mariner's adage: "Red sky at night, sailor's delight; red sky at morning, sailor take warning." Many had in fact heard troubling reports about a large storm brewing down in the Caribbean. But that was far away, hundreds of miles to the south, and since no order had come to evacuate their homes, they saw no real cause for alarm. They felt safe inside their long rows of tightly shuttered shelters built on poles high above the water line.

Just across Caillou Bay a few miles offshore, the tiny island resort of Île Dernière—or Last Island, to the English-speaking population—was gearing up for its biggest social event of the season, the ballroom dance. Hundreds of wealthy planters and tourists from all across the South had descended on the popular island for the occasion. Men, women, children, and servants had settled comfortably inside the grand hotel and its surrounding cottages in anticipation of the upcoming gala.

That morning, a few revelers out on the beach noticed something peculiar about the tide. The water seemed glassy, yet a series of choppy waves kept breaking higher and higher up the flat beach. Each time the breakers tumbled ashore, the frightened bathers and strollers backed playfully out of harm's way. They felt a trifle foolish, of course; that is, until they saw the mysterious mound of dark water forming far out at sea, about where the horizon line of the ocean collided with the cloudless sky.

Soon the beach began filling up with people wanting to know what all the commotion was about. Even at that early hour, they came dressed in their holiday finest—white coats and straw hats, hoop skirts and bonnets. Whenever their parents weren't looking, children carrying buckets and shovels scampered cautiously down to the water's edge.

Far out at sea, the monstrous wave seemed to be getting closer. The reddish glow in the sky had given way to grim overcast conditions. A light rain started falling, but mysteriously stopped before the first umbrella could be popped open. Seconds later, the sun broke back through the clouds.

The vacationers' fear gave way to fascination. Fascination soon dissolved into collective frustration—frustration that their wonderful seaside vacation might be interrupted by a silly storm!

Then, just as they were getting ready to trudge in and pack for a hasty ferry ride across the bay back to the mainland, the ominous wave subsided and the surf returned to normal. The people breathed a sigh of relief, then went on about their business, frolicking arm-in-arm down the glistening white strand.

What they couldn't see, and certainly wouldn't want to have seen, was at that moment a massive wheel of wind, wave, and cloud whirling furiously through the Gulf of Mexico. Mountainous walls of water rose and fell, collapsing against each other like tumbling skyscrapers, only to reconstruct themselves and fall again seconds later. Shrieking, clawing gusts of tropical air ripped at tattered clouds and spumes of spray and foam. Howling, moaning, hissing and hooting, the angry black storm churned steadily northward toward Île Dernière.

In those long, hot days before the Civil War, Last Island was the most fashionable and popular vacation resort in the South. Islanders especially liked to boast about their grand hotel— one of the biggest and most luxurious buildings in the Southeast. The sprawling two-story structure, surrounded by tennis courts, lawns, and flower gardens, could accommodate more visitors than any hotel in New Orleans.

Each summer the handful of permanent islanders—mostly farmers and fishermen—saw their population swell to nearly five hundred. That was just fine with most of them, because the influx of wealthy vacationers meant money in their pockets and spicy entertainment from sunset to dawn.

After dinner, merrymakers would gather in the grand ballroom to dance, drink, and eat until the wee hours. Concert music and recitals were provided by some of the top orchestral groups and individual performers of the day. Legend has it that on calm nights alligators and muskrats on the mainland bayous would crawl out of their swampy dens to listen to the sweet sounds floating over the bay waters from Last Island.

Ironically, the tragedy that would soon unfold on Last Island could have been averted. Had the islanders only paid heed to the signals—the strange, choppy surf, the eerie, whistling wind, and the clouds that seemed to gleam radiantly one moment, then dissolve into reddish puddles of fog the next— they could have climbed aboard the passenger ferryboat *Star* anchored behind the hotel and sailed away to safety. But later that night, while the waves rose higher and the winds grew stronger, the spirited vacationers preferred to dance their cares away.

The first to recognize that something was dreadfully wrong was the captain of the *Star* himself. Captain Abraham Smith had been around too long, weathered too many blows, not to sense that this was no ordinary storm. Why, he wondered, didn't the hotel authorities evacuate its occupants?

Even as his ship began to rock and grind dangerously against its moorings, he knew they still had time to climb aboard and make it across the bay to the mainland. If they waited much longer, it would be too late.

But they waited. And waited. The waves rose higher and the moaning winds became a tempest, a seething, slashing fury that blew into oblivion umbrellas, beach chairs, and anything else not tied or bolted down. Recognizing the danger, Captain Smith ordered his men to lash themselves to the deck. Seconds later, a powerful gust ripped his ship away from the marina. As the ship careened wildly away in the darkness, Smith knew it was every man for himself—and pity the poor devils on Last Island.

When the storm finally hit land, the first things to go were the crude fishing cottages and huts of the locals. Roofs, wrenched from walls, flapped away into the night like bat wings. Entire walls evaporated, along with carriages, barns, armoires, and shoes. Driven by the tempest, fenceposts and uprooted trees darted through the tumultuous darkness like missiles, striking and killing and destroying whatever got in their way—people, livestock, and other houses.

Only when a handful of terrified islanders rushed into the hotel did the music and dancing inside stop. Only then, when the orchestra had quietened down, did the gaily attired crowd hear the roar of the wind, the rumbling hiss of rising waters. Too late, the doomed men and women understood the extent of their danger.

Moving quickly to keep the crowd from panicking, the hotel managers spoke reassuringly about reinforced walls, stout timbers, and a strong roof. They explained that the unique design and construction of the hotel made it virtually hurricane-proof, that there was absolutely nothing to worry about, and that they should go back to the dance floor. Drinks and sandwiches were served on the house.

Sometime before midnight, as the smoke-filled ballroom reverberated with the brassy strains of the orchestra, someone saw a window full of water. She screamed. The music stopped and everyone watched as the dark, surging wall of debris-choked seawater strained against the delicate glass. Then, to their horror, they realized that water was rising above every window in the room!

At that moment, the huge building began to shake. The crystal chandeliers swung and jangled wildly, dishes rattled off food-bedecked tables, and guests began toppling to the heaving floor. The tall French windows disintegrated into jagged shards before the giant, crushing wave. Floor, walls, windows, and ceiling reassembled into surrealistic patterns, as bodies and furniture were swept outside into the marina and away into the sea.

All night long the storm pounded away at the island. Across the bay, along the marshy deltas of the mainland, people knelt and prayed inside their relatively secure homes for the poor souls out on Last Island.

Of the estimated four hundred people registered at the hotel that night, only forty survived the storm. Had it not been for the courageous actions of the ferryboat captain, who risked his own life to pluck dazed and bewildered survivors from the churning waters, it is probable that no one would have escaped.

When it was all over, nothing was left of Last Island—not a house, cow, or tree. In fact, the powerful storm had literally ripped the narrow island into two separate land masses. A deep channel, carved out by the killer storm that night in 1856, now flows between the two "last" islands—over the same spot where once stood the grand hotel.

The Carolina Bays:
Did an Ancient Comet Strike the Earth?

FOR YEARS, PEOPLE living along the Carolina coast have marveled at a series of oval-shaped depressions in the ground
called "Carolina bays." From the air these shallow, marshy
depressions and quivering sinkholes create a landscape that
resembles the pock-marked surface of the moon; they criss-
cross each other in a chaotic tapestry. At ground level they are
hardly noticeable, swallowed up by gloomy forests and lush,
semi-tropical swamplands. Highways and modern housing
developments have obliterated thousands of the bays, leaving
them visible only to trained eyes.

It is estimated that no fewer than 300,000 such bays, ranging
from a few feet across to almost two miles in diameter, dot the
East Coast landscape from southern New Jersey to northeastern Florida. One source places the number at more than half a
million. Few people outside the Carolinas have ever heard of
the baffling depressions, apparently because the largest number of them are found in North and South Carolina—hence the
name Carolina bays.

For hundreds of years the bays went unnoticed. The first
white man to record notice of them was John Lawson, who, on
an expedition down South Carolina's Santee River in 1700,
wrote about a "prodigious wide and deep swamp" where
there grew in great numbers a "tall, lofty Bay-tree, not the
same as in England, these being in their Verdure all Winter
long." Lawson called these gloomy regions "pocosins," an
Algonquin name for bay-covered swamps. "Bay swamps," or

simply "bays," remained the designated name for these formations as subsequent white settlers moved into the virgin back-country.

On his wilderness trek to Florida, naturalist William Bartram wrote in his journal about the botanical wonders of the bays. Accompanied by his son John, he took time to explore several large bay lakes, including Waccamaw, the largest extant Carolina bay lake. In 1847 the state geologist for South Carolina, an Irish-born gentleman named Michael Tuomey, evaluated the bays' significance: "A peculiar feature of this sand-hill region is the number of circular depressions that are scattered over the surface," he wrote. "They are not deep and conical . . . but flat and shallow, at first reminding one of a circular race course. They have quite an artificial appearance."

Interest in these "artificial" bays continued to increase as the region became more populated. Numerous theories were advanced to account for the mysterious formations, some admittedly fanciful.

One of the most intriguing early suggestions was that immense schools of fish, now extinct but once resembling salmon and shad, had created the bays as spawning grounds in prehistoric times when a shallow sea covered much of the Atlantic seaboard. Another asserts that the depressions are actually the marks of ancient icebergs that grounded and melted in the warm seas tens of thousands of years ago.

It wasn't until 1933, however, that a couple of professors from the University of Oklahoma issued a radical new theory to explain the Carolina bays. According to Melton and Schriever, they are actually scars left by a "meteoric shower or colliding comet." After years of study, the scientists concluded that "since the origin of the bays apparently cannot be explained by the well-known types of geological activity, an extraordinary process must be found. Such a process is suggested by the elliptical shape, the parallel alignment, and the systematic arrangement of elevated rims" of the bays.

Today, the cosmic-strike theory is widely accepted among scholars and is the standard interpretation offered in textbooks and journals. In his book *The Mysterious Bays,* Henry Savage draws a vivid picture of the rain of fire that fell from the sky ages ago to create the Carolina bays:

> These half-million shallow craters represent the visible scars of but a small fraction of the meteors that fell to earth . . . when a comet smashed into the atmosphere and exploded over the American Southeast. Countless thousands of its meteorites must have plunged into the sea beyond, leaving no trace; while other thousands fell into the floodplain of rivers and streams that soon erased their scars.

The bays' appearance bears out this theory. From the air they resemble peculiar elliptical depressions, or oval craters, surrounded by low banks of earth—or rims—invariably elevated at the southeastern end. Each bay's long axis extends from northwest to southeast, suggesting that the comet or shower of meteorites struck from the northwest at an angle of 35 to 55 degrees. Melton and Shriever believed that meteorites streaking in from the northwest at such an angle blasted into the relatively soft earth, leaving elliptical outlines upon impact. The sand blown away by the strike created rims and would "account for their accentuation in the direction of the strike." The meteorites would have struck with terrific force; it has been estimated that a single falling meteorite striking the earth at ten miles a second would be about equal to nineteen times the explosive energy of its weight in nitroglycerin. The impact must have occurred some time during the Ice Age, because the bays contain considerable buildup of fossil-laden sand and silt which indicates that the region was covered by the sea during the terrace-forming glacial period.

Many of the physical scars from meteorites are long gone—eroded by water, wind, and shifting sands, or simply vanished beneath the foundations of modern buildings, shopping centers, and highways. Some remain, however, visible from low-flying aircraft: low, egg-shaped depressions resembling gigantic flat coins, scattered over acres of fields, streams, hills, and woodlands.

The Lost Sea

THIRTEEN-YEAR-OLD BENJAMIN SANDS of Sweetwater, Tennessee, had known about the cave all his life. Ever since he could remember, his father had taken him on arrowhead hunting expeditions inside the dark, gloomy hole in the mountain known locally as Craighead Caverns. On Saturday afternoons he and friends would slither through the cave's narrow entrance and scamper down the slippery rocks inside until they reached the bottom. There they would play among the weird stone formations and gushing underground streams.

It was on such a Saturday afternoon in the summer of 1905 that the Tennessee farm boy discovered a tiny opening in the back of the cave. Lantern in hand, he eased into the cramped, muddy passageway, squirming along on his stomach until finally emerging, dripping wet, on the other side of the rock wall. His wildest fantasies had not prepared the boy for what he saw. "It was like another world," Sands would later write. "I knew at that moment I had discovered another world deep within the earth."

Glistening in the dim light of his lantern was a vast underground lake. In the inky shadows the crystal-clear water sparkled like cut glass, stretching as far as he could see. The cave room itself was so big and the body of water so broad the light from his torch was swallowed up long before reaching the ceiling or far side of the lake. For the rest of his life, Sands delighted in describing how he threw mudballs as far as he could into the unearthly blackness, listening to nothing but unseen splashes echoing through the still, vaulted chamber.

Although he couldn't have known it at the time, Sands had discovered the Lost Sea, the largest underground lake in the world, according to *The Guinness Book of World Records*. The lake, which is about 800 feet long and 220 wide, is actually part of an extensive and historic cave system.

For millions of years the five-acre lake had been hidden from the outside world. While mastodons and saber-toothed tigers stalked through primeval forests overhead, the waters of the Lost Sea had flowed in total darkness. The only life forms known to have flourished in the lake were large rainbow trout, whose three-foot-long descendants still thrive in the cold waters. Today, these sightless fish (whose eyes did not evolve due to the total darkness of their habitat) glide eerily through the lucid depths, resembling torpedoes suspended in watery space.

One of the cave's first visitors was a giant Pleistocene jaguar whose tracks have been found deep inside the cavern. According to Lost Sea records, the cat, which weighed 500 pounds and measured eight feet long, apparently lost its way in the darkness about 20,000 years ago and fell into a crevice. Some of its bones, discovered in 1939, are on display in the American Museum of Natural History in New York. Others, along with plaster casts of the tracks, are among the exhibits at the Lost Sea's modern visitor center.

Known regions of the cave have been used since the days of the Cherokees, who held tribal council assemblies and ceremonial rites deep in the interior. Nearly one mile from the entrance, in a room now known as the Council Room, a wide range of artifacts has been found, including arrowheads, pottery, and jewelry.

Ever since the first white settlers pushed into the area, there had been rumors of a large body of water hidden somewhere inside a local mountain. But nobody—not even the Indians—knew for sure. These rumors probably referred to the backwaters of a large spring running through the cavern, and not the actual lake itself. Officials at Lost Sea Inc., the company which now owns and operates the underground lake, believe the

Cherokees "conceivably" could have known about the lake, but there are no records of any human's having seen it until Sands's discovery in 1905.

In the early nineteenth century, white settlers used the cave as a kind of colonial deep-freeze, having discovered that their produce would stay fresh longer in the cool air. The abundance of saltpeter (potassium nitrate) in the cave also contributed to keeping the vegetables fresh. During the Civil War, the cave was heavily mined for saltpeter, a principal ingredient in the manufacture of gunpowder.

In 1915 the cavern's owner built a large dance floor inside the cave after expanding the entrance. But the "cavern tavern" concept soon fizzled when too many intoxicated revelers started loosing their way—and footing—among the slippery foot trails leading in and out of the bleak, subterranean passage.

Some eighty years and two million visitors later, the Lost Sea is one of east Tennessee's biggest tourist attractions. The Lost Sea Inc. was formed in 1964. A year later, the first group of visitors was escorted through the caverns and across the lake in a small boat. Scientists, explorers, and curiosity-seekers from all over the world flock here each year to stroll along the lonely shores of the lake and to glide across the surface in glass-bottomed boats powered by electric motors. The caverns are particularly appealing to cave climbers, who often book months in advance for an opportunity to explore the more remote regions. Spelunkers enjoy prowling the depths of the cavern, never knowing what wonders might lurk around the next corner or just beyond the flickering shadows.

Deep inside the yawning darkness, where temperatures can suddenly plunge twenty degrees or more, time seems to be suspended. The landscape is the stuff of nightmares and Hollywood science fiction. There are constant surprises: one moment you are trudging straight across a narrow rock bridge, past strange geological formations; the next, out on the smooth, silvery lake, a dangerously long fish swims right up to your boat. The surrealistic imagery is now intensified by green lights submerged along rock walls just below the lake's surface. Boats, people, and fish seem to drift through time and space, while the hollow whisper of a tour guide's voice echoes strangely through the semi-darkness. On thirty-minute trips through the cave, visitors can observe at close range several displays of rare crystalline structures called "Anthrodites"— fragile, spicy-spelling clusters commonly known as "cave flowers," found in only a few caves around the world.

It is a spectacular place, and as the guide's reassuring voice reverberates through the heavy air, one is reminded of a passage in Jules Verne's classic tale of subterranean adventure, *Journey to the Center of the Earth:* "My hair stood on end, my teeth chattered, my limbs trembled," declared one of literature's most famous cavers upon entering the shaft of a volcano that would lead him on a perilous nether journey.

Today, no one knows just how deep or far back into the mountain the lake flows. Teams of divers armed with modern exploration equipment have probed visible portions of the lake, but accurate dimensions have been difficult to map due to dangerous undercurrents and forbidding geologic formations. Beneath the calm waters of the lake itself, divers have discovered an even larger series of rooms completely filled with water. More than thirteen acres of the lake have been mapped so far and still no end to the main body of water has been found. As exploration continues, so does the cavern's intrigue.

The Mystery of Rock Oven

DEEP IN THE rugged Altamaha River Swamp in south Georgia, only a few miles downstream from the Edwin I. Hatch Nuclear Power Plant, is a rock formation known locally as Rock Oven. The limestone ridge is punctuated by a series of deep, winding tunnels and caves, which are thought to have once sheltered an enigmatic tribe of Indians and might even contain treasures left behind by early Spanish explorers.

Tradition has it that the gloomy lagoons surrounding Rock Oven are haunted by the spirits of Indians who left behind subtle reminders of their mortal presence—beautifully crafted arrowheads, cooking utensils, and pottery. Oldtimers who have hunted and fished this region for years swear they've heard strange voices echoing through the woods, seen eerie green lights, and glimpsed the wispy forms of Indians dancing around the entrance of the cave. Some think that devil worshippers are conducting their rituals there. To this day, some people around these parts won't venture near the caves, even in broad daylight.

One such person is Benny Coursey, a commercial fisherman whose riverfront cottage is located a few miles upstream from Rock Oven. Coursey, who used to raft timber down the Altamaha River to the sawmills on the Georgia coast near Darien, said the Rock Oven place is haunted.

"There's something down there that's awful strange," he said late one afternoon. The ninety-year-old grandfather was sitting on his boat dock, tending to some fish traps set out earlier that day. A breeze drifted in from the river, rustling through the bushes alongside the steep, muddy bank. Coursey smiled as he spoke. "I've heard fellows tell me they've seen ghosts around those old caves. And heard voices, like babies crying or a woman screaming. Of course, that might have been a panther they heard, who knows? But what was it they *saw?"*

Dr. Ray Crook, an assistant to the state archaeologist at West Georgia College, said the swamp, where the Altamaha River winds through southeastern Georgia on its way to the sea, has never been properly excavated. "We don't know a lot about the area," Crook said. "To my knowledge, there's never been a professional archaeological investigation."

Generations of spook-hunters have sought unsuccessfully to unravel the secrets of Rock Oven. Hikers and amateur pot-hunters have dug, scraped, probed, and climbed throughout the wet, slippery chamber of rocks in search of clues to the cave's mysterious past. In spite of their efforts the mystery remains—who built Rock Oven? When? And why?

The huge limestone wall, which snakes across a low-lying ridge overlooking a lagoon leading to the river, was formed millions of years ago when most of south Georgia was covered by a shallow sea. According to Dr. William McLemore, a state geologist in Atlanta, Rock Oven itself appears to be about twenty-five million years old, based on the type of ancient marine organisms found embedded in the rock. Limestone is made up of seashells, coral debris, and other marine deposits and takes millions of years to form. "There are limestone units [like Rock Oven] scattered throughout the area," McLemore said. "Ninety percent of these formations are derived from ancient organisms."

A few miles up the river, just west of the sprawling nuclear power plant on the Appling County side of the Altamaha, a team of commercial archaeologists recently uncovered artifacts thought to be several thousand years old. A spokesman for the Altamaha Area Planning and Development Commission in nearby Baxley said the archaeologists found pottery shards, flint arrowheads, and other evidence indicating the presence of Indians at least a thousand years ago. But some fiber-tempered pottery also was discovered in the area, lending support to theories that Indians lived along the river as long as four thousand years ago—much earlier than originally believed.

Rock Oven got its name by the main cave's charred interior—evidence, say local residents, that Indians cooked meals there a long time ago. Yet history tells us little about exactly what native Americans these might have been. Early Spanish missionaries mentioned "secretive" Indians who hunted and fished the wilderness area along the river, but little else. They used to pass these Indians on their way up-river from the coast to the fall line near Macon, where there lived a powerful tribe that developed one of the most elaborate civilizations in the Southeast. Known as the Ocmulgee Indians, these aboriginals built massive earthen mounds and traveled far and wide until, with the coming of whites, they vanished.

But Crook said little more is known about the Rock Oven people, referred to as the "Tama" by neighboring tribes. "We don't know exactly who these Indians were or where they may have lived," he said.

In spite of the region's spooky reputation, the caves have long been a popular place for picnicking, hunting, and fishing. There is real danger, of course; rattlesnakes, moccasins, panthers, wildcats, and bear do inhabit the gloomy swamp. But scenic rewards make the rugged trek worthwhile—virginal stands of sycamore, sweetgum, bays, and pines; palmetto thickets, clusters of flowering tangles, and gushing streams. Locals believe that this wild seclusion probably prompted early Spanish missionaries and explorers to hide their treasure from British as well as Indian attackers. Buried amid the damp bogs and quivering pools of quicksand are thought to be gold-laden chests, weapons, and other valuables worth a fortune. To this day, no sign of the treasure has been found, but many believe it's only a matter of time until some lucky pot-hunter strikes it rich.

"One thing's for certain," said Coursey. "There's a lot of

things about this old place that we'll never know. If we did, it wouldn't be a mystery anymore."

Unearthly Oddities

Gifts from the Sky

STORIES OF DELIGHTFUL or not-so-delightful objects showering from the sky are as old as recorded lore; they have always had their skeptics and their hot defenders.

The first documented skyfall in the southern United States occurred on Friday, March 3, 1876, when bits of pleasant-tasting meat plummeted down onto the Kentucky home of Mr. and Mrs. Allen Crouch of Bath County. The portions measured up to four inches square and resembled fresh beef. According to a couple of volunteers who tasted it, the substance was "either mutton or venison."

The next year, on a hot Sunday afternoon in 1877, the city of Memphis, Tennessee, was caught up in a wave of hysteria when a rain of living snakes suddenly started falling over the downtown area. Thousands of reptiles, some measuring more than eighteen inches long, terrified eyewitnesses for several days until the snakes could be collected and destroyed. Special church services and prayer meetings were held following the aerial invasion, as scientists rushed to the scene from as far away as New York and Boston.

The mysterious "rain of snakes" was officially attributed to a freak storm that had sprung up over a nearby swamp, sweeping up the snakes and depositing them over the city. However, the official explanation failed to satisfy several pressing questions: Why did the storm gather only snakes, and not squirrels, rabbits, turtles, and other light animals that cohabit the swamplands with the serpents? Why was there no wind accompanying the snake-storm? Perhaps most puzzling of all, how was it that thousands of snakes fell from the skies that day, a number that in all probability exceeded the local population of serpents?

On August 31, 1886, the city of Charleston, South Carolina, was jolted by an earthquake that rattled buildings and caused local creeks to overflow their banks. Soon afterward, reports of "warm stones" falling from the sky went around town. Three of the incidents had happened in front of the local newspaper office. The shower of bricks had actually begun about an hour after the earthquake, lasting for several minutes with each occurrence. Reporters and editors arriving at work at 7:30 the following morning gave alarming accounts of how they had to run and duck to avoid being struck by another barrage of stones.

Another shower of "grape-sized" rocks fell outside the news building at 1:30 that afternoon. Personnel inside the news offices who witnessed the phenomenon agreed that the stones seemed to fall from somewhere directly over the building, striking the pavement with such force they gouged out huge holes.

In 1901, a flood of small catfish, perch, and trout poured over Tiller's Ferry, South Carolina, causing a mild panic in some parts of the rural community. Three years earlier, something described as a "sulphur rain" had fallen on Mount Vernon, Kentucky. The foul-smelling substance was found to be highly flammable.

Occasionally, skyfalls occur in perfectly clear weather in full view of witnesses. Such was the case on October 23, 1947, when a deluge of freshwater fish—largemouth bass, sunfish, hickory shad, and minnows—drenched the town of Marksville, Louisiana. Although some fog was reported in the area at the time, the weather was calm and visibility excellent.

The aerial assault in Marksville began about 7:00 a.m., just as residents were rising and going to work. At first they didn't know what was hitting them. The fish continued falling for several minutes, striking a number of people scurrying to get out of the way. According to a local newspaper story, the fish were "absolutely fresh and fit for human consumption." A few appeared frozen; most were merely cold, but very much alive.

Another incident in Louisiana rocked the state with excitement when, on July 12, 1961, carpenters working on the roof of a house in Shreveport had to take shelter to escape a bombardment of golfball-size peaches. Some of the workers said the peaches looked as if they were being "tossed" out of a large cloud. Town officials speculated that a strong wind had swept up the fruit and dropped them on the workers. However, the local weather bureau dismissed that possibility, saying the wind that day was not strong enough to transport peaches through the air.

One of the most bewildering episodes involving skyfalls in Dixie was reported in August 1962. Grady Honeycutt, a farmer from Harrisburg, North Carolina, had spent the afternoon fishing on a small pond near his farm. Just as he was getting ready to head home, he saw something strange streaking down from the sky.

Honeycutt, who had read a lot about meteorites, watched the shiny globe plunge into the shallow pond, causing a loud splash that nearly swamped his small boat. As soon as his nerves had settled, he paddled over to the spot where the ball of fire had struck the water and peered down.

Resting on a muddy bed about seven feet below his boat was a "round and shiny" object unlike anything he'd ever seen before. He later described the thing as "looking a lot like a bowling ball that glittered strangely." He also said it had short spikes protruding from its smooth surface.

Honeycutt wasted no time contacting the local authorities. By the time the sheriff arrived, however, the mysterious object had disintegrated into a "tangle of shiny wires." Next morning, army divers were brought in to search for missing parts. Nothing was found—except for a few strips of aluminum foil, the kind used by the air force to help distort radar systems.

The Honeycutt case was officially closed but placed in the "unsolved" file in the sheriff's office.

Flaming balls of fire zipping through the night sky; showers of living fish and snakes; "hot bricks" and hailstones the size of softballs falling from the heavens. What are we to make of these strange gifts from the sky? Explanations range from the scientific to the supernatural, from black holes and extra-dimensional connections to poltergeists and otherworldly mischief. Chances are we'll never know, and that's probably just as well. A wise man once said that explanations can be a dangerous thing—unlocking doors to secrets and mysteries better left unknown.

Human Torches or Fire from Heaven?

ON A CHILLY autumn afternoon in 1952, police were summoned to the home of an Algiers, Louisiana, man who neighbors suspected might be the victim of foul play. No one had seen 46-year-old Glen B. Denney, owner of a local foundry, in days. When a woman next door smelled smoke coming from his house, she feared the worst.

After forcing the door down, investigators made a grisly discovery. In the middle of the living room floor, heaped between two chairs, were the charred remains of Denney's body. Flames, so hot firemen had to don protective clothing to smother out the blaze, still engulfed the blackened corpse.

Nothing else in the room had been damaged by either smoke or fire. Except for the smell, the only physical sign of the conflagration was Denney's badly burned body.

An investigation was launched to determine the cause of death. If it was suicide, as some authorities initially speculated, the victim must have used a lot of kerosene or gasoline to create such an intense fire. But not a drop of combustible fuel was found in the house—not even a match, lighter, or cigarette.

It appeared that Denney had simply died, "struck down by a fire from Heaven," in the words of one witness.

"In all my experience, I never saw anything to beat this," commented Louis Wattingney, a special agent called in to investigate the case.

Twelve years later, in October 1964, 75-year-old Olga Worth

Stephens of Dallas, Texas, was sitting in her car in a parking lot outside a grocery store when witnesses saw her suddenly burst into flames. The former actress was dead before anyone could reach her. Police investigating the incident reported no damage to the car, not even to the seat where she was sitting. Nothing was found in the car that could have started the fire.

Three decades earlier, on a cold January morning in 1932, Charles Williamson of Bladenboro, North Carolina, was lying on the sofa listening to the radio when he suddenly heard his wife scream for help. His daughter heard the scream too, and together they rushed upstairs to the bedroom to find Mrs. Williamson on fire. Father and daughter quickly ripped off her flaming cotton dress with their bare hands. Mrs. Williamson had not been standing near any kind of flame, nor had her dress been in contact with any kind of flammable substance.

Two days later, a bed caught fire in the same bedroom, as did the curtains in an unoccupied room. Soon after that, a pair of Mr. Williamson's pants hanging in the closet burst into flames.

Arson experts were called in to investigate the bizarre series of "spot" fires which broke out over a five-day period. The results were inconclusive. A local newspaper stated: "The fires started, burned out and vanished as mysteriously as if guided by invisible hands. There has been no logical explanation."

For more than three centuries, coroners, police, and pathologists have been intrigued by the curious phenomenon known as "spontaneous human combustion," or SHC. The scientific world has been reluctant to accept seemingly indisputable evidence that incidents of spontaneous combustion in humans might have occurred. Invariably, such cases have been simply dismissed as "puzzling" or "unsolved." Occasionally an accusing finger is pointed toward the investigators themselves, charging them with careless or "not thoroughly sufficient" work.

Thoroughly sufficient or not, the fact is, more than two hundred well-documented cases of SHC have been reported since 1670, many of them occurring in the United States within the past five decades. According to studies made at independent laboratories and at several universities in the United States and in Europe, the fatality happens to people of all age groups and in all walks of life, but seems disposed toward elderly people who drink a lot of alcohol. In the early days, people who died by spontaneous combustion were believed to have brought on their own demise by drinking, dancing, committing adultery, or other licentious behavior. Their cruel fates were presumably divine retribution, sent down from heaven in a shower of holy flames.

One of history's most bizarre cases of spontaneous combustion occurred on July 2, 1951, when Mrs. Mary Hardy Reeser, a 67-year-old widow, was visiting her son and grandchildren in St. Petersburg, Florida. Dr. Wilton M. Krogman, a physical anthropologist and world-renowned expert on the effects of fire on the human body, called the Reeser case "the most amazing thing I've ever seen. As I review it, the short hairs on my neck bristle with vague fear. Were I living in the Middle Ages, I'd mutter something about black magic."

No one really knows what happened to Mrs. Reeser that morning in 1951. The best that can be said is that she somehow caught fire and died before she could get to a window or door for help. The worst, however, is that it must have been agonizing death, the cause of which will probably never be known. Based on reports by witnesses and investigating officers, here are the details:

Early that morning, a friend of the victim's had gone to the Reeser home to deliver a telegram. Mrs. Reeser's son, Dr. Richard Reeser, and his children had gone to the beach, leaving the elderly Mrs. Reeser alone in bed. When the neighbor, Mrs. Pansy M. Carpenter, knocked on the door, her knuckles were scorched by an intense heat radiating from within. Alarmed, she stepped back and called for help. Two painters working across the street heard her cries and ran over to help. Smelling smoke, they broke down the door and were immediately struck by a blast of hot air.

While Mrs. Carpenter called the fire department, the painters searched the house for Mrs. Reeser. She was nowhere to be found. Other than the smell of smoke and a scorched over-head beam, the house seemed to be free of danger.

When firemen arrived later, one of them made an astonishing discovery. In a corner of the den was a charred area roughly four feet in diameter. Within that blackened area were a number of chair springs and the ghastly remains of a human body—consisting of a charred liver attached to a piece of spine, a shrunken skull, one foot wearing a black satin slipper, and a small pile of ashes. The slipper belonged to Mrs. Reeser, as had apparently the foot protruding from the grisly pile of ashes.

Suspecting foul play, the family called in the FBI, along with top arson experts from the National Board of Underwriters. Tests conducted at the scene indicated it would have taken an enormous, white-hot fire to have incinerated the victim so quickly and thoroughly. A blaze somewhere in the range of 3,000 degrees Fahrenheit—the same temperature range used by modern crematoriums—would have been necessary for the bones and tissue in Mrs. Reeser's body to lose their shape.

The remaining slippered foot was a mystery in itself. How could an entire human body be so thoroughly incinerated, yet one of its feet scarcely singed by the inferno? Apparently the foot was unburned because it was outside the circle of inciner-ation. Mrs. Reeser had been known to suffer from leg pains, causing her to often extend her left leg out and away from her body. This extension, suggested forensic experts, probably prevented the foot from being consumed by the same fire that cremated the rest of the victim's body.

A number of theories were advanced to explain Mrs. Reeser's death. Lightning was ruled out, since there had been no electrical activity reported in the area that morning. One possibility, ventured an arson specialist, was that the woman had taken sedatives, making herself so drowsy she failed to realize she had set herself on fire with a cigarette. However, neither the gown she was wearing nor the chair she was sitting in was particularly flammable. Besides, there was not enough material available in these items to produce the intense heat necessary to reduce a human body to ashes.

Another speculation, that the fire might have been caused by some failure in the electrical system, was also ruled out by the experts: the fuse would have blown. Murder and suicide were also discounted. Eventually Dr. Krogman admitted defeat. In his official report he stated: "I have posed the problem to myself again and again of why Mrs. Reeser could have been so thoroughly destroyed, even to the bones, and yet leave nearby objects materially unaffected . . . ."

Nor could he understand the shrunken condition of Mrs. Reeser's skull: "The head is not left complete in ordinary burning cases. Certainly it does not shrivel or symmetrically reduce to a much smaller size. In presence of heat sufficient to destroy soft tissues, the skull would literally explode in many pieces. I . . . have never known any exception to this rule. Never have I seen a skull so shrunken or a body so completely consumed by heat."

A number of other physical causes for spontaneous combustion in humans have been suggested, including fireballs, lightning, internal atomic explosions, laser beams, microwave radiation, high-frequency sound, and geomagnetic flux. Intestinal gases are also known to be flammable; fats and oils, which the human body contains in abundance, make excellent fuels as well. Static electricity sometimes produces sparks that could, under certain conditions, set a body on fire.

But no model has yet been constructed to demonstrate the accuracy or reliability of such theories. The mystery of spontaneous human combustion's "fire from heaven" may never be solved.

Paul Redfern's Final Flight
and Other Vanishing Acts

ORION WILLIAMSON WAS not a rich man, but he had every-thing he wanted—a loving wife, a healthy child, and a good farm. He was proud, too, having worked hard to save up enough money to buy his little spread on the outskirts of Selma, Alabama, and now he planned to make something of his life. Early on a July morning in 1954, as he set off from the house to fix a fence on the far side of the field, he thought he was the luckiest man in the world. When he got to the gate, he looked back and saw his wife and child waving from the porch. "Be back before lunch," he shouted, waving back.

Those were the last words Mrs. Williamson would ever hear her husband speak. Seconds later, he vanished before her eyes, right in the middle of the field. As it happened, two neighbors riding by in a buggy had also greeted Williamson a split-second before he disappeared.

Stunned, the two men stopped the buggy and raced out into the field to investigate. They were joined by Mrs. Williamson, who frantically shouted her husband's name over and over.

"It's no use, Mrs. Williamson," one of the men said after searching for more than hour. "He's gone."

Later that afternoon, dozens of searchers combed the un-plowed field and nearby woods for the missing farmer. Blood-hounds were brought in, but their nosing around did not bring any luck. Newspaper reporters, including the young Ambrose Bierce, got wind of the story and conducted their own search of the premises. Bierce would later write about the incident in his short story "The Difficulty of Crossing a Field."

Orion Williamson had simply vanished from the face of the earth. Not a trace of him was ever found, not even the clothes he was wearing nor the tools he was carrying in his hands.

Twenty-six years later, on September 23, 1880, Williamson's disappearance was recalled when David Lang, a young farmer living near Gallatin, Tennessee, vanished before the eyes of his startled wife and two visitors who happened to drive up in a buggy at that very moment.

Lang had just left his house and was walking across a field to hitch up a mule for plowing. About halfway across the field, near the barn where the mule was corralled, he waved to the couple of neighbors approaching up the far side of the road. The two men in the buggy—Judge August Peck of Gallatin and the judge's brother-in-law—waved back.

A split-second later, Lang disappeared in full view of his wife and both men. Astonished, the visitors climbed down from the buggy and set out to search for the missing farmer. Lang's wife joined them, running first around the barn, then meeting the two men on the far side of the field. Thinking there might an unknown sinkhole or cave on the property, the trio continued searching until dark, then resumed the futile hunt the next day with several other neighbors.

As with Williamson, however, nothing was ever seen or heard from Lang again. He too had simply vanished.

Each year, thousands of Americans vanish into oblivion without a trace. In an age of computerized records kept from the cradle to the grave, it is difficult to comprehend how living human beings can suddenly and unaccountably fade or plunge into the unknown, leaving no trail or clue to their whereabouts. Of the estimated ten million Americans who are reported missing each year, about 95 percent eventually return or are accounted for within a few days. Five percent vanish forever.

Vanishing without a trace in the nineteenth century was one thing, but when wealthy, sophisticated people suddenly disappear in the middle of a modern American city in the 1980s, it's something else. Such was the tragic case of an elderly New York couple, who checked into a motel in Brunswick, Georgia, on the night of April 8, 1980, and were never seen again.

Charles R. Romer and his wife, Catharine, had made the long journey between their New York home and their apartment in Miami many times. They knew the route well, and often stayed over in Brunswick, the first overnight stop on the way. The Romers liked Brunswick, a bustling seaport city just across the causeway from Sea Island and St. Simons Island.

On the night of April 8 they checked into a local Holiday Inn along busy Highway 17. A little later a state patrolman spotted their black Lincoln Continental parked along the road near a cluster of restaurants. The officer theorized they were going to a restaurant for dinner.

If so, the couple never arrived. The Romers and their late-model luxury car simply disappeared.

In spite of a nationwide search, no trace of the couple was ever found. At first police considered murder as a motive, but since no bodies were found, there was no evidence to support the claim. One other possibility was kidnapping. Still, when neither the couple's car nor their bodies were ever discovered, investigators looked to other causes for their disappearance.

One baffled police officer suggested that the Romers had run off the road into a swamp while driving through the countryside. That theory seems highly improbable, however, since their suitcase and other belongings were left behind in the motel room.

Like Williamson, Lang, and others, Charles and Catharine Romer had simply vanished without a trace.

One spectacular disappearance in the South that stands apart from all others involved Paul Redfern, a young pilot from Sea Island, Georgia, whose ambition was to be the first person in the history of aviation to fly nonstop from the United States to South America. On August 25, 1927, his small, brightly painted monoplane, named *Port of Brunswick*, was loaded up with enough provisions for the long trip, and a crowd of several thousand onlookers gathered at the beach runway to see him off. Amid the fanfare, twenty-five-year-old

Redfern hunkered down comfortably inside the cockpit, waved goodbye, and taxied for takeoff. The pilot had to be in a fine mood that hot, humid August morning as his 5,500-pound monoplane skimmed along the beach, then lifted gently into the powder-blue skies over Sea Island. Down below was his wife of six months, along with several financial backers of the expedition and a swelling crowd of spectators. After a ceremonial dip of the wings, the *Port of Brunswick* droned off into the clouds.

Except for a few reports that his plane had been spotted flying on course over the Caribbean, then once more over the city of Ciudad Bolívar in Venezuela, nothing else was ever seen or heard of Redfern. He and his plane had simply vanished. Occasionally, reports still trickle in from the jungle claiming that the wreckage of Redfern's plane has been found, invariably in a remote, inaccessible region. As of this writing, no conclusive evidence has been forthcoming, in spite of hundreds of search party operations—including one led by the swashbuckling movie idol Errol Flynn.

One modern adventurer claims to know where the plane went down but says it would cost a fortune to reach the spot and retrieve the wreckage. "We're talking about true dinosaur country," said retired commercial airline pilot Robert Carlin, who has spent decades researching the Redfern story. "Steel wool jungle, pristine. Not even any Indian trails. . . . The plane was apparently hanging up in the trees for a great number of years. And I know the plane can be found. I could take you to the spot."

Redfern's destination was Rio de Janeiro, about 4,600 miles away from Sea Island, almost twice the distance of Charles Lindbergh's 2,500-trip from New York to Paris three months earlier. His flight plan was to take him from Georgia to the Bahamas, across the Caribbean and then over Puerto Rico, on past the tropical islands of Grenada, Tobago, and Trinidad, past the coast of British Guiana (now Guyana), and across Dutch Guiana (now Surinam) and northern Brazil to Macupa on the north bank of the Amazon.

Aboard his Stinson-Detroiter airplane, loaded down with

about 550 gallons of fuel, he carried a two-gallon container of drinking water, enough emergency food to last ten days, and complete survival equipment for ocean or jungle, including a pneumatic air raft, a small distilling outfit, mosquito netting, quinine, and a collapsible rifle and ammunition. Since radio instrumentation was not yet available, pilots in Redfern's day were alone among the clouds.

The mystery of Paul Redfern's final flight would soon be overshadowed by that of another ill-fated pilot—Amelia Earhart, who disappeared in 1937 while on a record-breaking round-the-world voyage. Like Earhart's last flight, Redfern's has found a lasting place among the unsolved mysteries of aviation history.

What happened to Redfern? Over the years, numerous theories emerged to account for his disappearance, many of them predictably fanciful. One had him crashing into a jungle and becoming head of a tribe of Brazilian Indians. Another said Redfern was captured by a hostile tribe that used spears to discourage rescuers from reaching him. Some reports said he was alive and well; others said he had been badly crippled by the accident, but chose to remain in the jungles rather than return to civilization.

Whatever happened, Redfern's widow finally gave up hope. Seven years later she had her husband officially declared dead. "If anyone had seen my husband and had been with him, as some of these people say, I would think he would have given them something to prove his identity."

South Carolina's "Healing Springs"

LUTE BOYLSTON LOVED the land. As a farmer, born and bred in the South, he saw the fields and woods surrounding his South Carolina homeland as God's gift to the people—a reward, he felt, for honest, decent folk who worked hard and led righteous lives.

It annoyed him when friends and neighbors abused God's gift. For years, the Barnwell County planter watched his beloved land slowly deteriorate—first from careless agricultural use, and later from the encroachment of civilization. When houses, shopping centers and parking lots began gobbling up great chunks of virgin territory, Boylston began to worry. Where would it all end? How much land would be left to his grandchildren? His great-grandchildren?

For years he stood helplessly by while developers, outdoor recreationists, and even other farmers pillaged the countryside. Then, one warm summer day in July of 1944, he did something a bit unusual to protect his farm. He climbed into his pickup truck and drove into town, stopping to collect his attorney and then heading to the courthouse to file a new property deed.

In that deed—still on file in the Barnwell County Courthouse—the 76-year-old farmer gave explicit instructions that upon his death part of his property would be deeded over to God. After all, reasoned Boylston, it had been God's land in the first place. In the unusual bequest he stated that he didn't believe "the white people who dispossessed the Indians ever

88

appreciated the value of God's will sufficiently to help in any way preserve for posterity this gift of God Almighty to mankind."

The piece of land deeded over to God happened to be the site of Barnwell County's famous "Healing Springs." For decades, men, women and children from across the country had been flocking to the springs to drink, bathe, and play in the cool, clear waters bubbling from the ground. Many of those who did so claimed the waters possessed miraculous healing powers.

Boylston himself recognized the divine power of the springs as well. In his deed of land to God, he made it clear that "the Almighty had intended the cool waters of the wells to be a source of comfort to the afflicted. . . . I return to Him the most treasured piece of earth that I have ever owned or possessed."

The farmer's princely act earned him a big blue and white sign posted beneath several huge trees and a granite marker beneath a clump of oak trees surrounding the springs. Waves of people continued to enjoy the springs, which now, officially, belonged to God—the only piece of land on earth legally deeded so.

Indians had been the first to know about the mystical little patch of ground. Local legends suggest some of these Indians worshipped the waters—or at least spirits in the waters. Early settlers drank from the springs as well, and the mystical tradition continued. During the Revolutionary War, soldiers often camped around the springs to rest, bathe, and—according to some accounts—help heal wounds suffered in combat.

By the middle of this century, the Healing Springs had become a favorite destination for thousands of travelers from all parts of the country—even Canada and Europe. Eventually the springs were named an official state attraction. (This well-intended act probably has old Lute Boylston turning in his grave.) On any given Sunday, gangs of visitors descended on the one-acre plot of land to sip from the springs and splash their faces and arms. They came armed with plastic jugs and glass jars, metal buckets and wooden barrels—anything that would hold the life-giving waters from the Healing Springs.

Inevitably, the garbage began piling up. Plastic candy and cigarette wrappers. Beer cans. Discarded human debris which occasionally reached unmanageable proportions. Boylston's quiet little spring in the woods, the spring he had returned legally to God, was rapidly becoming a dumping ground for human refuse. Ironically, many of the people who came to the springs for comfort and healing were the same ones causing most of the mess. In stepped the state of South Carolina. If Barnwell County didn't take action soon to clean up the springs, the popular tourist attraction would lose its official status.

Disgusted by heaps of debris left over by man and nature, groups of concerned citizens joined forces to restore "God's little acre" to its former pristine condition. Spearheaded by the local chamber of commerce, the cleanup campaign was a roaring success. Healing Springs regained favor with the state and is still a state tourist attraction. Thousands of people still come here each year to partake of the waters' mysterious properties.

One such visitor is Sammy Lee Dunn, who claims to have been making the 150-mile round-trip to Healing Springs for the past fifty years. The 82-year-old Saluda County retiree believes the spring water is filled with "the Lord's mysterious powers. It's in there. And I ain't about to quit coming as long as the Lord will let me."

Sounds from Beyond

RABUN COUNTY IN the northeastern corner of Georgia is one of the most ruggedly scenic regions in the southern Appalachian mountains. This is true *Deliverance* country, made famous in the early 1970s by novelist James Dickey and the movie by the same name. In the old days Rabun County was a remote, unspoiled place where adventurers could ramble for days without so much as hearing the sound of another human voice. Towns like Clayton, Dilliard, and Mountain City seemed cut off, isolated from the rest of the world, until modern roadways began slicing through these hills in the early 1930s. Then came the tourists, trickling up and down Highway 441 which winds through the Great Smoky Mountains. It was only a matter of time until the first row of condominiums popped up on the side of a Rabun County mountain.

But in spite of new condominiums, shopping malls, and superhighways, Atlantans' vacation homes and Floridians' retirement centers, a sense of wilderness prevails. There are still places in Rabun unmarked and unseen by human eyes. Certain backwoods trails lead toward remote ridges and caverns, unvisited for hundreds of years. Some who have ventured down such trails swear they just disappear—vanish into smoky mists rising from deep within the earth. Indian legends claim that fire-breathing demons once dwelt among these lonely hills and woods, and that "little people" or "little demons" stood guard over sacred caverns and curious stone

91

assemblies hidden in the forest. Occasionally, outsiders trekking through the backwoods report hearing strange sounds—sounds that over the years have come to be known as "music of the Bald."

For more than a century now, the music of the Bald has tantalized generations of Rabun Countians. According to those who have heard, the sound is less like music than like trees falling or boulders crashing far off in the woods. Some say it even sounds like cannon firing in the distance. A few, whose testimony has gone on record, swear the sounds are always preceded by screeching, or noises like babies crying in the night. Although they are most often heard at night, many people claim to have gotten an earful in broad daylight.

The first written account of the sounds appeared in an issue of the *Monthly Weather Review,* published in 1897. Two "reliable gentlemen" were reportedly camped on top of Rabun Bald, the highest peak in Rabun and one of the loftiest in the southern Appalachian range. About ten o'clock that night, they were awakened by sounds which reminded them of cannons being discharged in the distance. The booming noises went on for several minutes, echoing through the dark, lonely woods. Soon, however, they noticed that the sounds appeared to be issuing from the ground, from a ridge southwest of the mountain. According to the report, the men were perplexed, but "not badly frightened," even though at times the sounds seemed to proceed from the ground beneath their feet. At any rate, they sat up until the wee hours listening to the eerie booms.

When the two campers confronted the local sheriff with their experience the next morning, they were told that the sound might have been caused by bears rolling small boulders off the mountainsides in search of worms and snails. In those days, black bears were plentiful in Rabun County. Pioneers would often come upon the beasts pushing with their enormous paws and noses at rocks and boulders, apparently to get at edible goodies beneath. Sometimes the boulders would roll downhill or off cliffs, creating explosive sounds as they shattered on the rocks below.

The sheriff's explanation satisfied those two campers. But the sounds continued into the twentieth century, long after most of the bears had been killed off or driven to higher ground. Homesteaders sometimes were awakened at night by inexplicable noises. Hunters and trappers told about "eerie, haunting melodies" drifting through lonely glades and down the mountainsides. These sounds were attributed to the ghosts of two men murdered on Rabun Bald back in the late 1860s.

Scientists called in to investigate the noises generally attributed them to settlings within the ground, or boulders and rocks shifting on their own accord. As for the haunting screams heard by others, they were dismissed as screech owls or other wild birds and animals. Perfectly convincing, unless you happened to be the hiker who once felt the hot breath of "something evil and strange" on the back of his neck. According to a report by Barry C. Hawkins in the *Monthly Weather Review,* "some have heard these sounds so near them in the woods" that they had to run to escape a powerful presence that came over them.

Another enigma that has intrigued Southerners for years are the so-called "Seneca Guns": eerie booms echoing just off North Carolina's southeastern coast. These sounds, described as a cross between an earthquake and a sonic boom, usually are heard during daylight hours. Whenever they occur, houses shake, windows rattle, and nerves tingle.

Jim Lanier, director of the North Carolina Aquarium at Fort Fisher, says he has heard the sounds several times. He said, "It was pretty dramatic. It sounds exactly like artillery fire, artillery guns."

Investigations, however, have revealed no military activity in the area at the time of the sounds. Scientists called in to probe the phenomenon frequently point to another possibility—chunks of the continental shelf dropping off a cliff under the Atlantic Ocean. This latter theory is "a total misconception" of the shelf or the slope, according to Lanier, who has spent a lot of time studying the strange rumblings. "It's very gradual in this area," he said. "The continental shelf and the slope are quite gradual and there's nothing there that could break off and make this kind of rumbling noise."

But whenever buildings start shaking and windows start rattling for no apparent reason, a lot of local residents think it's time to call in a squad of ghostbusters.

"I hear it all the time," said Susan McClain, a dispatcher at the Southport Police Department. "There's no pattern. It's something between a sonic boom and an earthquake." Ms. McClain, who noted that the offshore booming has been going on since she was a youngster, said, "We've had people call and say it shook windows and knocked things off the shelf. Some days it's heavier than others."

Even Lanier admits the noises are a mystery.

"We had a funny instance where they had been going off a few times, and it sounded like one morning that someone had been rolling heavy equipment over the exhibit room floor," he explained. "There was a rumbling and you could feel the building shake, just slightly, not alarming, but the way it would shake when a jet broke the sound barrier. Of course people go and check it out and no jet broke the sound barrier in the area and the military disclaims any knowledge of any explosions going on and then people start speculating about what it is."

The mysterious noises have never been reported after dark. Some locals who claim to have heard the sounds numerous times don't recall ever having heard them on a Sunday either. Could it be that the good Lord may not want to disturb things on the Sabbath Day?

That's a question a lot of people would like to answer.

But answers—comforting answers, anyway—appear to be no nearer today than they were when the first odd sound was reported earlier this century, to the dismay of people living along the coast. "It's a little frustrating for all of us in that we don't have an explanation for it," said Lanier. "Under those circumstances, it's understandable that there's a lot of misinformation around."

At least one official believes that whatever is causing the offshore noises is also causing the beach to erode. "Ever since that started, this beach has been going," huffed Roby Osborne, police chief in Long Beach.

Screams echoing across a lonely mountaintop in Georgia, and eerie rumblings off the North Carolina coast; these are only two of the more disturbing phenomena in nature's storehouse of mysteries in the South.

The Man Who Wouldn't Die

YOUNG WILL PURVIS had proclaimed his innocence all along. In court he swore he was nowhere near the Mississippi farm owned by a man he was accused of having murdered the previous year. So when the jury returned a verdict of guilty, Purvis was stunned. He dropped to his chair, rubbed his head, and began softly sobbing. When the judge asked him to rise for sentencing, Purvis turned toward the jury and in an icy tone said: "I'll live to see the last one of *you* die!"

On February 7, 1894, the sheriff came to take him to the gallows. It was a gloomy day, but even the threat of rain couldn't keep away the 3,000-plus spectators gathered on the courthouse lawn to watch the hanging.

The sheriff, a burly fellow toting a shotgun, escorted Purvis up the rickety flight of steps leading to the hastily erected gallows where a hooded hangman and a preacher waited. A light rain had begun to fall and Purvis watched waves of umbrellas pop out in the huddled crowd below.

Some of the onlookers waved. A few fought back tears as they watched the doomed man trudge across the scaffolding. Many still believed him innocent. As the noose settled over his neck, Purvis whispered to the priest: "I am innocent of this crime. I did not kill anyone." With that, the trapdoor swung open and wide and Will Purvis, gagging and kicking, plunged into space. For a few horrible seconds the crowd gasped while his 140-pound body twitched and fluttered on the end of the thick rope.

But suddenly Purvis's body crashed through the platform to the wet earth below. Above his head, swaying in the chill afternoon breeze, was the rope. It had apparently come unknotted during the hanging, allowing the condemned man to slip through. On the ground below the gallows, Purvis picked himself up. Aside from one small cut on his cheek and some bruises around his neck and shoulders, he was unharmed.

For several seconds the crowd was quiet. Then a low murmur began to sweep through the pressed ranks, followed by whistles, clapping, and cheers. "We knew you were innocent," shouted several in the crowd.

But the sheriff, a stern-faced man clad in a large gray overcoat and wide-brimmed hat, was unimpressed. He had been hired to hang a man, and hang he would. Without further ado, Purvis was led back up the steep flight of steps to the scaffolding a second time. A thin trail of blood trickled down his cheek as he stood over the trapdoor, waiting for the noose to be reknotted and placed over his head.

But the crowd had seen enough. Convinced they had witnessed a miracle—and of the young man's innocence—the entire audience began singing, shouting hallelujah and praising the Lord. They demanded that the prisoner be released.

Utterly bewildered, the sheriff consulted with the clergyman for a moment, then reluctantly led Purvis back to his cell.

"Don't get any funny ideas. We ain't done yet," the sheriff snarled in Purvis's face.

In the weeks following, attorneys for Purvis launched a barrage of appeals with the Mississippi State Supreme Court, but to no avail. A new execution date was set for December 12, 1895. Purvis's friends, however—and many others who had witnessed the "miracle"—had other ideas. A few nights before the scheduled hanging was to take place, a group of disguised men and women stormed into the jailhouse, tied up the sheriff's deputy, and escaped with the prisoner. Warrants were issued for his re-arrest, with a bounty this time, but Purvis was nowhere to be found.

For months the young outlaw remained in hiding, confident that a new governor would be sympathetic to his cause. When a new chief executive was finally elected later that year, the now-famous fugitive turned himself in. Instead of being treated like a criminal, however, he found a hero's welcome.

Thousands of letters had poured into the state capitol demanding a full pardon for the crime Purvis swore he didn't commit. Toward the end of 1898, almost four years after the date he was to have hanged, an official pardon was issued by the governor.

Twenty years later, a dying man named Joseph Beard confessed to the murder of the Mississippi farmer and Will Purvis was finally exonerated.

The story doesn't end there, however.

During his trial in 1894, Purvis had told the jury repeatedly that he was innocent, that to send the wrong man to the gallows would be a mortal sin. When his pleas had fallen on deaf ears, he vowed before the judge to outlive them all, just to prove his innocence.

On October 13, 1938, twenty-one years after his exoneration, Purvis died—three days after the death of the last juror.

Specters And Spells

Miracle in the Clouds

ON THE AFTERNOON of August 15, 1988, a crowd of about twelve thousand gathered on the grounds of a small Catholic Church in Lubbock, Texas, to witness a miracle. For days they had been drifting in from all corners of the globe. Some brought sleeping bags and tents to stay in while awaiting the event, while others arrived in four-wheel drive vehicles and sleek motorhomes. The occasion was the Feast of the Assumption, one of the Roman Catholic Church's holiest festivals, which celebrates the day the Virgin Mary ascended into heaven. But this was to be no ordinary celebration of the feast.

Television cameras and reporters swarmed among the worshippers. Helicopters buzzed overhead. A small contingent of police had been stationed nearby, just in case they were needed. In the midst of the congregation stood Monsignor Joseph James, charismatic leader of the St. John Neumann Catholic Church, a huge underground structure located on the outskirts of town.

Breathlessly the people waited. Necks craned toward the heavens. Many wept and prayed. Others recited prayers on their knees, from the back of pickup trucks or from lounge chairs. Even above the roar of helicopters and the murmur of the crowd, the rattle of rosary beads could be heard.

The fact is, nobody really knew what to expect. They had been told only that something "miraculous" was going to happen on the church grounds soon, probably on the sacred day itself. Monsignor James had prepared his people well.

After a trip to Medjugorje, Yugoslavia, a few months earlier, he had experienced visions of the Blessed Mother of Jesus, and he was confident that she was at last going to reveal herself to his congregation—at least in signs, if not in spirit. At regular services during the past few weeks, hundreds of worshippers had heard fellow parishioners transcribe special messages—messages from the Virgin Mary which supposedly had come to them in a series of prayer-induced visions. Hastily scribbled down in the notebooks of parishioners, these words had come to a selected few who knelt on the altar as the congregation recited the rosary.

"My dear little children," one of the messages said. "Listen to me, your mother. I want to help you. I want you to be in Heaven, where we can pray and serve our father for all eternity. Yes, my dear ones, you must have signs and you will have these signs . . . but it will be up to you to believe."

Another message promised salvation to the pure of heart and to those who believed in the messages: "My children, do not be sad. Have joy in your hearts, have peace. Listen to the prayer that you ask for, the Lord will give it to you."

Most of the supernatural utterances were received by three regular churchgoers—Mike Slate, a retired air force officer; Mary Constancio, a former hospital therapist; and Teresa Werner, a housewife and mother. The three recipients would reportedly go into a trance following several minutes of prayer by the congregation, then automatically begin "receiving" the holy communication while fellow parishioners looked on in reverent silence.

When news of the messages broke, thousands of believers rushed to the church to see the miracle for themselves during regular and special services. The church wasted little time capitalizing on the series of reported miracles. More than fifty thousand books containing the messages were rushed off the presses and into circulation throughout the South. Plans were being made for additional volumes as the number of visitors swelled. Promises were made that a major miracle would occur soon. Many churchgoers, including the Monsignor, believed that all the signs pointed toward August 15, the annual celebration of the Virgin Mother's miraculous ascension into the clouds. As wire services and newspapers picked up the story, followers from around the world began making plans to attend the heralded manifestation. At one point it was estimated that at least thirty thousand people would descend on the little church to witness the miracle that the faithful believed would transform their lives forever.

August 15 was a warm, muggy day, but a breeze stirred through the chanting, singing crowd. One newspaper reporter said there "was electricity in the air. . . . You could almost sense something great was about to happen, even though in your mind you knew it wouldn't. Still, you wanted something to happen—anything, an unusual cloud formation to develop, a freak thunderstorm, a hailstorm, even a tornado. Anything to kindly reward these patient, God-fearing people."

Sometime during Mass that afternoon someone spotted a strange cloud high overhead. Then another. And another. Soon several unusual cloud formations seemed to come together to form a portrait of Jesus. A few seconds later, some of the astonished onlookers recognized the holy face of the Virgin Mary herself riding high in the clouds.

A calm prevailed as thousands of trembling fingers pointed skyward and faces grew warm in the glow of the late afternoon sun. Many in the crowd claimed that the sun appeared to dance in the sky, while multicolored lights and shadows played in the shimmering clouds. Some in attendance that day swore that their silver-colored rosaries turned a golden hue.

Whatever it was that had happened that warm August day in Texas, it was over in a hurry. No one heard the rustling of wings or the blaring of trumpets; not a single person in the crowd claimed to have been "illuminated" or caught up in any special rapture. There were just the faces in the clouds that seemed to smile down for a few seconds, then dissolve into a spectacular display of lights.

Many—especially those who had driven far and were probably doubtful anyway—were disappointed. But for untold thousands of others, those who wept and prayed and cried out for signs from their heavenly redeemer, the signs had been there. They had seen the face of Jesus in the clouds, along with that of the Virgin Mary. They were convinced they had witnessed a miracle. Some people reported that their ailments mysteriously cleared up. Bob Golec, who journeyed to the service from Midlothian, Texas, said his chronic knee problems disappeared after Mrs. Werner relayed a message from Mary to him and the church pastor included his name in a healing prayer.

Maybe it was mass hysteria that caused the collective "visions," as skeptics were quick to point out. But what caused the color change in the rosaries? Who could explain the overwhelming sense of calm that prevailed in those few dramatic minutes while more than twelve thousand people watched and waited—then observed—what they firmly believed were divine wonders?

Immediately following the August 15 feast, a panel of Texas bishops was appointed to study the charismatic church and its reports of miracles. Lubbock Bishop Michael Sheenan asked the National Conference of Catholic Bishops to assist him in investigating the event. But a spokesman for the conference in Washington said the organization would stay clear of such a probe.

"He [Sheenan] is free to set up his own investigation and ask experts in on his own, but the national organization [prefers to have] nothing to do with that," said Joe Lipovsky.

Sheenan, who called on Monsignor James not to continue promoting or printing the books until the investigation was concluded, warned that people shouldn't assume anything supernatural ever happened at the church.

"I take a cautious attitude about the rosary messages spoken about by several parishioners at St. John Neumann," he said a month before the feast day in August. "I neither encourage people to participate in the events nor do I discourage them."

Voodoo and the Walking Dead

INTO THE NEW World they came, untold thousands of them, not as conquering heroes or divinely charged pioneers, but as simple slaves and servants to work the fields and woods. They came from the west coast of Africa, kidnapped from their villages and rounded up like cattle, then packed aboard cramped, disease-ridden ships for the long voyage across the ocean. Chained, shackled, and beaten into submission by their white overlords, these unfortunate souls were forced to draw upon secret inner strengths if they were to survive the horrors of the southern plantation.

Such secrets had been handed down from generation to generation, along with other customs, traditions, and ancient tribal beliefs.

One of those secrets was the mystical power of Voudou, or voodoo, as it came to be called in America. In time the practice of this enigmatic religion, blended with elements of the Roman Catholic faith, would become the dominant religious force among transplanted Africans in the South. Voodoo offered hope and the promise of supernatural rewards to its gangs of followers who often congregated in the dead of night.

No one really knows how voodoo became so widespread in the Southeast, especially near New Orleans in the eighteenth and nineteenth centuries. The religion, which focuses on the magical powers of a serpent god kept in a box, was first prevalent in Haiti, probably brought over from Africa's Slave Coast. Eventually it was introduced to slave communities living in the southern United States, where it took root and blossomed.

In a world of unspeakable hardships for African slaves, voodoo provided its followers a badly needed spiritual outlet. While practicing their age-old faith, slaves as well as later generations of free blacks could suspend their troubles, if only temporarily, and concentrate on a world beyond. Often that world was not so divine. Frequently, it became a place of unrelenting horrors, a nightmarish realm suspended somewhere between reality and the imagination.

Today the ancient religion is still celebrated in song and dance. Its arcane practices have been the subject of numerous television specials, and practitioners, in a sense, have become celebrities in the wake of frequent appearances on talk shows and interviews in major newspapers and magazines.

Spells are still cast, curses are frequently heard, and the mystical protection of charms remain a fundamental part of traditional voodoo enclaves in the South. Just as they did in the old days, voodoo kings and queens see to it that their "favorites" receive all the protection they need from evil spirits, while blasphemous enemies are dealt with accordingly through powerful mumbo-jumbo and an occasional sacrifice.

The word "voodoo" itself has long been enough to conjure up sensational images of naked, writhing bodies dancing wildly around a roaring fire, enraptured by the steady beat of drums and chanting worshippers. Such scenes often depict trance-induced dancers swirling around with increasing frenzy until finally they collapse, moaning and groaning, to the ground. Snakes are usually shown hissing and coiling around attractive young women, while muscular, half-naked men dance and gorge themselves with the bloody entrails of mutilated sacrificial animals.

Practitioners of voodoo insist that such cinematic treatments of their ancient art are not far from the truth. In fact, say some who have observed or participated in the ceremonies, movie-makers would be shocked at just how accurate many of their celluloid portrayals actually are.

Sacrifices—human and otherwise—were not uncommon in

the early days, and whispers of blood-letting ceremonies are still heard in the bayou backcountry of Louisiana and Mississippi. Chickens and roosters are usually the preferred sacrificial animal. Blood smeared on the floor and on the lips of worshippers who sit cross-legged in a circle is seen as one of the secret ingredients needed to unlock the doorway to a variety of mystical powers.

Of all the voodoo queens in New Orleans, none was more feared nor respected than Marie Laveau, a large, mustachioed woman said to have the devil's strength and an angel's charm. Laveau, who reigned as the supreme voodoo queen during the years of the American Civil War, possessed extraordinary powers of conjuration. On St. John's Eve, the most sacred of all spectacular voodoo celebrations, Laveau would retreat to a hidden bayou along Lake Pontchartrain. Crouching before an altar, the mulatress would clutch a serpent and chant:

> "L'Appe vinie, li Grand Zombi
> L'Appe vinie, pour fe gris-gris!"
> ("He is coming, the great Zombi
> He is coming to make gris-gris!")

Then into the clearing would leap a tall Negro brandishing a small black coffin. At the sight of him the celebrants, gathered around a cauldron seething with witches' brew, would bound into the air, screaming, "Li Grand Zombi! Li Grand Zombi!" At the conclusion of the chant, the contents of the cauldron— live pigeons and chickens torn limb from limb—would be distributed until faces and teeth and hands and bodies were smeared with blood. Then the voodooists would dance and whirl and scream until many fell to the ground unconscious.

Public pressure targeted against such bizarre rituals eventually drove voodoo underground. Voodoo ceremonies, though still common, are today a closely guarded secret. It is hard, though not impossible, for the uninvited to witness a ritual. In New Orleans and other cities in the South where there are large concentrations of blacks, one may buy the same kinds of charms and powders and lotions used in Laveau's day. If you know where to go, there are stores offering Love Powders, Get-Together Drops, Boss-Fix Powder, Easy Life Powder, Come To Me Powder, Devil Oil, Controlling Oil, and Dice Special.

Many educated blacks—and whites—are still careful not to cross anyone said to be possessed with an "evil eye"—a strong indication that person is a sorcerer or enchantress and is likely to be equipped with the skills necessary to cast powerful spells at will. Foremost among those to be feared are the voodoo kings and queens and their representatives.

Today, voodoo rituals take place in private homes, in the middle of dark forests or swamps, on street corners, and even in cemeteries. Followers of the ancient religion believe that by heeding a list of strict rules, they can summon and win the favor of a particular *loa,* or god. Loud, exotic ceremonies are usually required to get the loa's undivided attention, hence the pulsating dancing, singing, and music-making at regular rituals.

However, smaller requests can be made in the privacy of one's own home, simply by purchasing or assembling a charm and by following a list of grisly instructions from the head queen of a region. Even today these queens are both respected and feared for their far-reaching supernatural powers. Such powers enable them to conjure up spirits to punish or reward, depending on the circumstances, and members of a voodoo community see to it that they always remain in good favor with the Head Queen.

Most voodoo practices today are curious blends of Old World rituals and established Christian teachings. Congregations sing Protestant hymns accompanied by clapping hands and stamping feet. Members "fall out" and "talk in the unknown tongue" while church leaders summon the ghosts of departed relatives and heal ailments. Many church leaders do a brisk business in gris-gris on the side.

No discussion of voodoo would be complete without mentioning zombies, dead people called back from the grave by either a priestess or priest called a *houngan.* These nightmarish creatures, whose souls have been stolen by the houngan, are reanimated as mindless robots—zombies—and are required to follow its creator's instructions. Belief in zombies, or the walking dead, is a central feature of voodoo and was the subject of a recent popular movie, *The Serpent and the Rainbow.*

Despite their history of suffering, African-Americans have contributed much to New World culture: backbreaking labor, ingenious skills, and wonderful customs, artistic works, and inventions. But not all these gifts have been sunny and straightforward. Voodoo must be counted among them—one of the more mysterious and macabre strains of the ancient, proud black heritage.

The Surrency Haunting

WAY DOWN IN south Georgia, in a railroad settlement on the edge of the Altamaha River Swamp, people talk about the Surrency ghost as if its reign were only yesterday. But it was more than a century ago, in the late 1870s, that the hotel-home of the Allen Surrency family—the family for whom the town was named—became center stage for one of the most spectacular hauntings in American history. In less than a decade, news of the strange goings-on at the Surrency home had spread all across the country, with thousands of journalists, scientists, and curiosity-seekers pouring in to investigate.

Diaries, books, newspaper and magazine reports, and hundreds of personal accounts vividly describe the unearthly activities that occurred in that old house: tables and chairs flying through the air, mirrors exploding in hallways, clocks running wild, hot bricks raining from the sky, mysterious lights flickering in the dark, and the noises—bloodcurdling noises ranging from sorrowful weeping to sadistic bursts of unexplained laughter.

Only a handful of oldtimers are still around who actually saw the house; fewer still are alive today who witnessed the spooky manifestations before the structure went up in flames early one Sunday morning in 1925. Those who remember speak nostalgically of their town's infamous ghost, pleased at the attention their community once received.

Phillip Dukes, who ran a local grocery store until his death in 1985, did not believe in ghosts. But in an interview with an

Atlanta newspaper right before he died, the elderly Surrency native said he didn't "doubt for a moment" the veracity of accounts handed down to him from his grandmother. "She used to spend the night at the house often, because she was Mrs. Surrency's sister. A lot of times when she put her shoes under her bed at night, she'd wake up next morning and find them out in the hallway. That happened so many times she came to expect it every night. She never figured out what caused it, so she thought it must have been the ghost."

The late Hershel Tillman, a longtime postal carrier for the Surrency district, was also convinced that ghosts were responsible for the haunting. As a boy he visited the Surrency house many times, but it was stories related to him by his father, uncle, and other relatives that convinced him there was more to the Surrency ghost than just talk. "No doubt about it, a ghost was involved," Tillman said. "I wasn't old enough to understand, but the poor people who lived in that house always had trouble going to sleep once the ghost invaded the place."

Nearly every person in town has his or her own tale about the Surrency ghost—tales invariably handed down from grandparents or great-aunts and -uncles who had visited the house in times gone by. Most stories center around the mischievous activities of a poltergeist—a restless spirit that supposedly derives pleasure from wreaking havoc in the lives of its mortal hosts.

According to Rev. Henry Curtiss Tillman, the supernatural forces haunting the Surrency house rarely disappointed visitors. Tillman said his father, the late Eason F. Tillman of the Ten Mile Community near Surrency, often described how plates, cups, and saucers would dance on the table at mealtimes, bedcovers would roll up and down at night, and glowing red lights would hover over the railroad tracks directly in front of the two-story house. "My daddy was one of the most honest men who ever lived," Tillman said. "When he said he saw those things, he really saw them."

Newspapers during the late 1800s and early 1900s were full of disturbing stories about the ghost, many written by journalists who visited the house and witnessed firsthand the sightings they recorded. Appearing in the *Savannah Morning News* on October 28, 1872, was an article purporting to be a "reliable report of the mysterious Surrency phenomenon."

A reporter had arrived at the Surrency home by train late one afternoon, and had just settled down for a smoke and interview with his hosts. As he scribbled notes on a pad, his attention was drawn toward a large, handsome wall clock in the parlor.

The clock was hanging on the wall in the parlor, and had ever been characterized by the correctness of its time. Suddenly with a weird, buzzing noise the hands began moving around with exceedingly rapid motion, the hour hand exactly five minutes ahead of the minute hand. In this singular position they continued to move for seventeen minutes, in which time it had described five hours and each time as it arrived at the twelve o'clock mark, it would pause and strike, one hour for another, such as twelve for one, etc., and at the end of the five hours ceased its wild movements.

The same writer told of books mysteriously falling off the library shelf, bottles of oil leaping off a table and onto the floor, fire logs rolling repeatedly out of the fireplace, hogs suddenly appearing in the living room, and unearthly screams floating down the lofty old corridors. "The whole thing is clothed in darkness and . . . bears the spirit of the supernatural," the writer concluded.

Eager to rid their home of their unnatural guest, the Surrency family sought the help of scientists, ministers, mediums, and psychics. The hauntings coincided with a wave of interest in psychic phenomena sweeping the country and Europe, and the twenty-year period before the close of the century was the heyday of "spirit investigations," including such celebrated cases as the Fox Sisters' séances. Mediums had become as popular as modern athletes and movie stars, and more than a few "specialists" were brought to Surrency to investigate the ghost.

Efforts to drive away the ghost—or ghosts—were unsuccessful, however. If anything, they seemed to make matters worse. Windows suddenly began to shatter at random, doors refused to stay closed—even when locked—and scissors and irons flew across the room. Perhaps the eeriest phenomenon is described in the following article from the *Baxley News Banner*:

> On the day of the ghost's first appearance, Mr. Surrency had gone to Macon to purchase some supplies. A minister who was visiting in the home that night and one of the older sons were sitting in a room when they heard a loud thud on the front porch. The boy got up and went outside to see what was happening, and discovered the noise was caused by bricks falling on the porch, and he also found they were hot.

Another shower of hot bricks descended on the Surrency home later that same night.

In the months and years that followed, similar incidents continued. Relatives and neighbors took turns staying with the Surrencys, partly to lend moral support and undoubtedly in hopes of witnessing the events themselves. An estimated twenty thousand people visited the haunted house during those troubled years, the majority of them given free room and board by the Surrency family.

Tradition has it that a murder was behind the Surrency hauntings. One story tells of a trunk that was found in a bedroom, stuffed with a corpse. Another points to Allen Surrency himself, charging the wealthy landowner and farmer with foul play in the death of a man who once had owned the property on which the house stood. One surviving witness, who wished to remain anonymous, described Surrency as a "sick, sadistic fellow possessed with sorcery-like talents." The witness recounted how Surrency had once supposedly demonstrated his arcane powers by running a broom twig completely through his head without spilling a drop of blood!

Some investigators theorized that the disturbance at the Surrency house could be explained scientifically. An unusually large magnetic field was believed to be located beneath Surrency, possibly triggering physical reactions. A more modern explanation centers around a peculiar geologic formation situated in the earth's crust nine miles below the town limits. Geologists suspect this formation, known locally as the "bright spot," might be an ancient reservoir formed more than 500 million years ago by the collision of the North American and North African continents.

Internal pressures from this subterranean pool of fluid, trapped for millions of years following the awesome collision, conceivably could be responsible for strange physical phenomena, such as the baffling events at Surrency. "It might have something to do with Surrency's ghost," thinks Mayor Stanford Tillman.

For years, until the fire put an end to its controversial existence, the Surrency house stood as a landmark next to the Southern Railway Line that splits the small town. The house served both as home to the Surrency family and as a hotel for overnight train travelers.

In those days, before the turn of the century, Surrency was a bustling little town full of promise. Its position on the railroad line, plus its booming naval stores industry, assured the town of continued growth into the twentieth century. But that was not to be. Baxley, ten miles up the road, soon took the lead, and Surrency's population began rapidly declining. Today, fewer than five hundred people call Surrency home, and the crossroads community is little more than a ghost town.

In the beginning, the Surrency family was terrified by the ghost occupying their home. On many nights it was impossible to sleep in certain bedrooms because the beds would "hop up and down like rabbits," covers would fly off the bed and dangle in the air, and articles of clothing would mysteriously disappear, only to be found weeks later at the same spot where they went missing.

Gradually, however, family members grew accustomed to the eerie antics of their visitors from beyond. But when they moved to another house not far away, the ghost went along.

Hershel Tillman, who watched the old house go up in

flames early one Sunday morning in 1925, said: "That thing haunted Old Man Surrency until the day he died. But when he was buried, the haunting stopped."

And what became of the ghost?

In an interview with the *Atlanta Journal* in 1929, Hampton W. Surrency, brother of Allen, said its own popularity probably contributed to the phenomenon's demise.

> It is a mystery. We might almost say that it was killed by too much popularity. People came from everywhere to see it. The railroad advertised its presence and ran special trains at tourist rates to bring visitors to Surrency. The village was small, and hotel accommodations were not sufficient to care for such large crowds. My brother realized the danger, and knew that it would ruin him, as he was a very hospitable man who made every effort to assure comfort to the multitudes who came.
>
> So he decided to move to another farm he owned six miles out in the county. . . . The ghost was never again seen at the big house. It appeared to have vanished as suddenly and mysteriously as it had come.

Fin, Fang,
And Fantasy

The Sea-Maiden of the Biloxi

ENCOUNTERS WITH STRANGE sea creatures were nothing new to Robert Froster, a thirty-five-year-old professional scuba diver from Australia. Over the years the Aussie had tangled with sea snakes, sharks, poisonous eels, barracuda, and even a giant manta ray. Still, none of his adventures had prepared him for what came charging at him through the clear blue waters of the South Atlantic one afternoon in 1988. Although he survived without a scratch, the ordeal has left him with emotional scars and a deep fear of the sea. Since the incident he refuses to go back into the water.

It all began with a request from a friend to help explore and photograph some strange rock formations several miles off the coast of Florida. Froster had probed the shallow continental shelf there several times before, because he too believed that the mysterious undersea formations might be the ruins of an ancient city—perhaps even Atlantis.

On this particular afternoon, however, Froster was diving alone. He knew he was violating the most sacred rule in his dangerous business—always dive with a buddy—but when his companion had been unable to accompany him on the trip, he decided to go it alone. It was a decision that nearly cost him his sanity—and his life.

Everything had been going fine until he noticed a disturbance in the water behind him. When he turned to look, he saw a vague, shadowy figure slashing toward him. All around him the water had begun to churn wildly, and clouds of sediment were swirling.

He knew it wasn't a shark; the creature was too lean, too lithe. As it rushed toward him, it appeared to undulate, rather than glide directly like a fish. When the fast-moving form got within twenty yards of him, he noticed something else odd about it. Appendages, like arms, seemed to be reaching out toward him, and at the end of each arm appeared to be sharply taloned hands.

Seconds later the creature came into full view. That's when Froster saw the unmistakable pair of breasts, long flowing hair, smooth skin, and scaled tail from the waist down. Froster nearly dropped his mouthpiece.

"The thing came straight at me," he told a Florida newspaper. "It was a mermaid, all right—half woman and half fish, with female breasts and upper torso and a fish-like tail below. That creature had one thing on its mind—to kill me because I had seen it. I've never seen such evil hate in the eyes of any human or animal before."

Before the apparition could reach him, however, Froster shot up toward the surface. Several times before he reached the boat, he thought he felt the curl of cruel talons on his flippers and ankle. Fortunately, he was able to scamper over the side of his craft to safety. He never saw the creature again.

"But it's still down there, I suppose, guarding the secrets of that ancient city," theorized a bewildered Froster.

Froster's amazing confrontation with what he believes was a mermaid resembles other encounters reported by sailors, divers, and swimmers down through the years. Legends about mermaids, or mermen, exist in nearly every country and culture in the world, from landlocked desert kingdoms to communities along inland rivers as well as on the coast.

In most tales, they appear as beautiful young men or women whose haunting melodies, when heard ringing out over the waves of lonely rivers or the ocean, are usually interpreted as a sign that danger or death is at hand for listeners. They are rarely friendly to humans, except when trying to lure them to their doom.

The fact that no flesh-and-blood mermaid or merman has

been captured or washed ashore on some uncrowded beach does not diminish the possibility of their existence, at least in the eyes of believers. However, scientists who have studied the phenomenon have offered some plausible explanations, ranging from manatees and sea-cows to seals and floating pieces of driftwood. Seen lolling near the surface or flippering along through the waves, these sea creatures and objects often bear an uncanny resemblance to human forms.

One of the most famous descriptions of a mermaid in southern waters was provided in 1614 by Captain John Smith. Upon spotting the strange creature, Smith said the "upper part of her body perfectly resembled that of a woman, and she was swimming about with all possible grace near the shore." His meticulous observation continues: the sea-beast had "large eyes, rather too round, a finely shaped nose (a little too short), well-formed ears, rather too long, and her long green hair imparted to her an original character by no means unattractive."

Like sea serpents, the legendary mermaid, whose enchanting beauty and powers of seduction most certainly have kept her in our favor down through the ages, figures prominently in our literary and artistic record. Plays, poems, books, movies, and other significant works of art have been spawned by our fascination with this mythological wonder-beast. Once exposed to its mystical lure, one cannot escape seduction, whether far out at sea or landlocked in a library or movie theater.

In Louisiana, legend has it that an entire Indian tribe—the Biloxi, also known as the Pascagoula—marched into a raging river at the command of a mermaid-like sea-goddess and drowned. True or not, the fact is that the Biloxi Indians did suddenly and inexplicably vanish during the early sixteenth century, only weeks after a white, bearded priest had appeared to them with a crucifix in hand demanding that they abandon their superstitious belief in an underwater goddess.

The Biloxi lived on the banks of the River Pascagoula between New Orleans and Biloxi, Mississippi, and worshipped a beautiful mermaid deity, whose statue was housed in a handsome temple. On moonlit nights they held rituals at river's edge while listening to the sweet stirrings of the mermaid's music. The music was said to be so sweet that brave warriors would weep under its spell. Sometimes the men would dance adoringly around the goddess's sacred idol while womenfolk played strange instruments to accompany her bewitching sound.

But sometime in the year 1539 a Catholic missionary came to dwell among them and attempted to turn them against their pagan ways. Apparently the priest had some success, because eventually the peace-loving Biloxi tore down their temple and threw their idols into the river.

Not long afterwards, according to tradition, the river-goddess rose from the boiling depths and, amid a towering column of waves and the sound of rushing water, commanded her people to join her in paradise.

"Come to me, come to me, children of the sea,
Neither bell, book, nor cross shall win ye from your
   Queen."

Unable to resist her siren call, the Indians went into a frenzy. Around the flickering flames of a ceremonial bonfire, they danced and drank and shouted out their ancient goddess's name. Then, one by one, they plunged into the murky river and perished. The next morning, there was not a single man, woman, or child left in the land of the Biloxi.

Even today the Pascagoula is known as the Singing River, because according to a newspaper writer's account, on warm, summer nights "people hear a low humming coming from the river," as if hundreds of voices were chanting in unison below its waters.

The legendary mass suicide of the Biloxi tribe has intrigued historians and archaeologists for years. There is some evidence suggesting such a mass extinction, but a few scholars theorize the action came not from the mythological summons of a water demon but at the hands of a more powerful tribe, perhaps the Choctaw. Romantic versions of the story insist, however, that it was the haunting lyrics of a mermaid that drove the Indians to their watery deaths.

Some experts who accept the mass-suicide theory have linked the tragic episode with that of another, equally baffling case involving a group of African slaves freshly arrived in Georgia. Although no mermaid was involved, the story of the Ibo tribe's mysterious fate on St. Simons Island is equally fascinating.

According to a tale circulated among black Seminole Indians in Florida, the West Africans had been en route to Charleston when they made a stopover at St. Simons, a sizable coastal island near Brunswick. While there, the shackled slaves some-how learned of the fate awaiting them at the hands of white plantation owners in South Carolina. In slavery, they would no longer exist as human beings. Families would be split up, perhaps never to see one another again.

A great sadness prevailed over the hundred or so Africans that night as they pondered their uncertain future aboard the cramped, disease-ridden vessel. Finally, a tall chieftain stood up and announced he had a plan. Rather than submit to a life of bondage, the proud Ibo tribesmen should take their own lives.

The chief's radical proposition was not immediately well-received among the Africans. When the chief assured his subjects, however, that happiness and freedom awaited them in "the world beyond time," the tribe decided death was better than slavery, especially if they were all going to be together with their loved ones in paradise.

So beneath a pale, full moon they marched, the entire group, their chains clanking and clattering in the muted southern night, and the echoes of their soft chanting ringing through the gloomy oak forest along Dunbar Creek. One by one they shuffled into the swirling depths of the creek, and one by one their black, naked bodies vanished beneath the waves.

Nowadays condominiums and a waste treatment plant are located along the creek where the Africans are said to have drowned. But on still summer nights, when the moon is shining bright over Dunbar Creek, islanders claim they can still hear the rumble of low chanting and the grind of metal chains echoing beneath the waters.

●

Behold the Fanged Serpent

NATIVE AMERICANS PROBABLY invented tall tales about giant rattlesnakes to enhance their own religious experience. Over time, these myths became part of the their belief system. Winged serpents and hissing water demons existed at the top—and bottom—of early American religious pantheons, and in between was their symbolic, though very earthly agent, the fanged rattlesnake.

The first Europeans to arrive in the New World heard terrifying tales about these strange creatures. Rattlesnakes the size of trees were said to lurk in the southern swamplands. Reports of snakes large enough to swallow a man whole were not uncommon.

Such exaggerated accounts were in all probability spawned by local Indians who resented the encroachment onto their lands by these pale-skinned strangers. The stories were intended to frighten gullible explorers, traders, and settlers hacking their uninvited way through the wilderness. Their impact upon our ancestors cannot be measured, of course. But for anyone huddled around a smoldering campfire in the wilderness or the flickering embers inside a lonely log cabin, the tales must have been effective.

Gradually, the mythological rattlesnake became ingrained in our folk tradition. As more and more settlers poured into the virgin wilderness, tall tales about rattlesnakes began to get even taller. Each harrowing encounter seemed to become even more harrowing with embellished treatment. Overblown accounts eventually reached all the way back to the relatively civilized coastal regions, and from there even to the courts of England.

For example, the story is often told of the unfortunate home-steaders in Kentucky who happened to build their cabin on top of a snake den. Soon after settling in, the pioneers built a glorious fire and began celebrating their new way of life with a housewarming. But that night, as the story goes, thousands of warmed-up rattlesnakes issued forth from the ground and caused what must have been no little consternation in the occupants.

Such incidents could have really happened. Rattlesnakes do occasionally den up in large numbers, and it is just possible that cabins and houses could have unknowingly been erected on top of an underground nest. However, the "cabin over the den" legend probably began when a couple of rattlesnakes slithered innocently through some cracks into a house, under-standably startling the owners.

By the late 1700s it had become almost impossible to sepa-rate myth from reality. Snake lore seemed to grow as fast as the young territory, and no region of the South lacked bone-chilling tales about monstrous aggressive rattlesnakes. Size figured most predominantly in these stories.

In 1714, for example, several rattlers were killed that were longer than 17 feet.

In 1750, a rattler killed in Virginia was said to have stretched to 18 feet.

In 1753 a group of traders killed a rattler that measured 22 feet—minus the head and rattles. The snake had reportedly attacked without provocation before it was killed with several musket balls and a well-thrown hatchet.

In Mississippi, a man swore he was chased by a 16½-foot-long rattler that he had mistaken for a dead tree. In 1872, a Georgia farmer couldn't believe his eyes when he saw a snake, which he thought to be a rattler, stretched across the two-lane road—a distance of about 15 feet.

The mangled carcass of a giant rattlesnake struck by a train in Washington County, Alabama, reportedly had 53 rattles and measured 13 inches across the middle of its body. The *Dallas Weekly Herald* of July 28, 1877, reported that an 18-foot-long rattlesnake had been killed in the Cherokee Nation, near Eufaula. "Thirty-seven distinct rattles" were on its tail.

More recently, the *Texas Game and Fish* magazine ran a story in October 1954 about a "giant rattlesnake" that measured just over 11 feet long "without its head and rattles."

Even today, newspapers and magazines occasionally carry articles about huge rattlesnakes that have either been spotted or killed—usually in a garden behind the house or crossing a highway. These stories may be accompanied by a black-and-white photograph of a portly farmer or hunter holding the dead snake up by the tail for all the world to scrutinize. Rarely, however, do we find the outlandish, diabolical dimensions reported by our ancestors!

Why? What happened to the giant serpents of old? If you ask a herpetologist, the answer is usually simple: stories about rattlesnakes longer than eight or nine feet are just that—stories. Some time in the past, for reasons already discussed, it probably became fashionable to "exaggerate" the size of snakes, especially rattlesnakes. After all, it's only human nature to stretch the truth—as well as the snake hide—a wee bit every now and then. Cowboys bored from a day out on the range, or explorers weary from their travels through wilderness, were certainly not above spinning a good yarn whenever the situation called for it—such as when a tenderfoot happened to be bunking down nearby. A three-foot rattler that slithered inside a sleeping bag might somehow become a ten-foot killer; a coiled serpent at the back corner of a barn might turn into a forked-tongue monster packing fifty rattles and a button.

Such embellishment was usually harmless, of course, perhaps even therapeutic in a rough-and-tumble sort of way, but over the years reality became fuzzy.

The size and aggressiveness of rattlers were only a part of the snake lore rapidly seeping into frontier consciousness. Yarns about other snakes, even harmless varieties, began to flourish around rural country stores and barbershops.

The hoop snake of the southern United States, for example, is alleged to have attacked unwary travelers by "rolling" into them and pricking them with its tail. It supposedly accomplished this miraculous feat by scooping up its tail in its mouth and twirling along like a hoop after its intended victim. Within striking distance, it released its tail and hurled its body—tail first—inflicting a deadly sting with the tip.

Another much-maligned creature was the coachwhip snake, said to have been another vicious attacker in Southern folklore. This speedy snake was supposedly faster than a horse, and once it caught its victim would stick its head inside his mouth so he couldn't scream, then proceed to "whip" the hapless individual to death with its tail. The mature coachwhip snake, which can grow to five feet and more, apparently earned its name because its streamlined body resembles a slender, braided whip.

Along the marshy streams and ponds of the Southeast lives the much-feared cottonmouth moccasin, so named because, when frightened or agitated, its "cotton-white" mouth opens wide to reveal a set of glistening, deadly fangs. Although cottonmouths do not grow very long—three to four feet is the average length—they often exhibit aggressive behavior, and will attack even if unprovoked. Many are the woeful stories about careless victims wandering into the squirming coils of these creatures, hanging from tree limbs and bushes in the swamps. Fishermen wading along riverbanks are particularly careful not to disturb these easily annoyed snakes, whose bite can kill or cripple.

No account of snake lore in the South would be complete without mentioning the legendary black racer, rumored to be the fastest snake in the world. Every boy who grew up on a farm has his own story about these long, lithe serpents that prey on mice and birds around barns and old houses. Also known as black snakes, these swift reptiles are said to be able to keep up with a car going thirty-five miles per hour! Ironically, the black snake is one of the rattlesnake's closest companions. During hibernation, it's common to find dozens of these non-venomous reptiles coiled up inside a den alongside their more dangerous cousins.

It is easy to understand the human fascination with snakes. They are creatures both lovely and loathsome; the sight of them can strike terror in the hearts of many of us, while others regard them as a blessing in our rodent-plagued ecosystem. We like to talk about snakes. At any zoo, the snake department is always the most popular. Yet ask any one of us to touch a snake—that is, actually reach inside a cage and pet one, even a harmless grass snake—and watch the reaction. Invariably it is one of repulsion, revulsion, and unrelenting fear.

Too, we are intrigued by the unique physics of their earth-bound form—flickering tongues, glassy eyes, sinuous coils, venom-dripping fangs. At the same time, we see them as the essence of evil, possessed with mystical powers that go beyond mere rat-catching dynamics. After all, didn't Satan tempt Eve while in the guise of a serpent in the Garden of Eden?

But snakes—especially rattlesnakes—seem to trigger within us all some deep, emotional antipathy—a chilling response that harks back perhaps to a time long ago when our barefoot ancestors shared the earth with these great lords of the forest floor.

The Shadow of the Beast

ON THE NIGHT of June 10, 1988, seventeen-year-old Christopher Davis was driving through Scape Ore Swamp, a dismal bog near Bishopville, South Carolina. It was late and the boy was tired, having moments before driven his date home. He was heading east along the narrow road when he heard a pop, then felt the car lurch out of control to the right.

A flat, he groaned, dreading the thought of having to stop in the middle of the swamp to change the tire. Not that he was afraid; he knew these woods like the back of his hand. He and his buddies had fished and hunted these parts since he was a kid.

But as he pulled his car off the edge of the road, he did feel suddenly alone. And afraid. It was way past midnight, with not another car in sight. The moon was high, but dark, gloomy shadows pressed in from the deep woods, scattered every few yards by moonbeams. Stepping outside the car that night was like stepping into another world—an uninviting world of shifting shadows.

Then Davis realized how quiet it was. There was no sound, not even the chirp of a cricket or the croak of a bullfrog. That's odd, he thought, popping the trunk open and hauling out the spare tire and jack. Usually this time of night the swamp was jamming with all kinds of grunting and groaning. Why was everything so quiet?

He didn't like it.

To calm his nerves he started whistling. It was a hot, humid night, typical for that time of year, but a pleasant breeze stirred through the moss-draped oaks and pines. He pulled off his shirt and slung it inside the car.

Dead, he thought. Maybe everything in the swamp was dead. Maybe some toxic nerve gas or other chemical junk had been dumped into the swamp and all the animals had belly-upped beneath the lily pads.

It was only a joke. But somehow he didn't feel like laughing.

He worked quickly, first removing the flat tire, then replacing it with the spare. At the back of his mind was a wish—that he could see the headlights of another car approaching up the highway. That would be a welcome sight. He vowed never to complain about traffic again.

The tire changed, young Davis wiped his hands and looked around before stepping back into the car. That's when he heard the noise off in the woods. A shuffling sound, like that of a large animal dragging itself slowly toward him through the bushes. He was reminded of the sound skin divers make when they try to walk on dry land with flippers.

Swish! swish! swish!

Without a flashlight it was impossible to see what was making the noise. Not that he really wanted to. But something had come over the boy, and he found himself unable to move. Large drops of sweat broke out on his forehead and the palms of his hands felt like jelly. He stood there for several more seconds, glued to the spot, listening to the swishing sound advance steadily closer. His heart was pounding inside his chest like a jackhammer. Sweat poured down his face.

Then he saw the creature. It stood less than ten feet away from him, a tall, slimy hulk that looked like some kind of weird cross between a man and an ape. In the pale light of the moon, Davis estimated the thing stood at least seven feet tall and appeared greenish-black.

For several seconds boy and beast stood on the lonely highway at the edge of Scape Ore Swamp staring at each other. The boy was the first to move. He moved fast, leaping into the car and slamming the door shut behind him. Mercifully, the car's engine roared to life. As it did, the creature sprang.

"It was strong and it wasn't an animal and it wasn't no man," Davis later told Sheriff Liston Truesdale.

The lizard-like monster first grabbed the door, then started banging on the roof. Frantically, Davis put the car in gear and accelerated, the creature hanging onto the hood. Davis had to swerve several times along the road before the creature finally lost its grip and tumbled off the car into the dark. To the young man's horror, however, the thing managed to keep pace with him at about thirty-five miles per hour.

Davis's ordeal was the first known encounter with South Carolina's now-famous "Lizard Man." It was not to be the last. In the days and weeks that followed, dozens of other people reported seeing a large, reptile-like animal loping through the rugged woods and fields of rural Lee County, South Carolina. Most of the sightings occurred in or near Scape Ore Swamp, a particularly gloomy region which got its strange name in Revolutionary War days. According to one legend, the name was shortened from Escaped Whore Swamp, so called because a group of British soldiers had escaped from an American ambush there.

Most descriptions of the monster matched Davis's, down to the "red eyes, lizard-like skin, and greenish-black color." One farmer near Brownville said something resembling the creature broke into his hog pen and "caused all kind of ruckus" before he chased it away with a shotgun blast. The thing he saw had a long, thick tail which it used to help climb over a fence and escape. There were bloodstains all over his hog pen the next day.

The "Lizard Man" of Brownville, as the creature soon came to be known, spread terror throughout this rural region as more sightings were reported. Sheriff's deputies were pressed into round-the-clock action as alarmed citizens began stocking up on guns and ammunition. Investigators combed the county for clues, escorted by volunteer hunters armed with high-powered weapons.

Before long, the entire country knew about the monster. Network television crews swarmed into town, along with reporters for national newspapers, magazines, and wire services. Everybody from Seattle to Seneca wanted to know more about the monster said to be haunting the lonely Lee County countryside.

But what was it? Nobody seemed to know. There were theories, of course, many of them wilder than descriptions provided by eyewitnesses. Explanations ranged from the plausible to the fanciful. Some said it was a bear. Others insisted the thing had to be an escaped gorilla. A few thought it was a hoax—maybe a man, decked out in a weird outfit, going around scaring people for kicks. At least one investigator claimed the monster was another Bigfoot, the legendary ape-man said to roam the higher elevations of the Pacific Northwest. The description did match those of recent "Bigfoot" sightings in other southern states, notably Florida, Georgia, Louisiana, North Carolina, and Alabama.

One of the most incredible accounts came from Florida in the mid-1970s when a deputy sheriff by the name of Joe Simboli reported an encounter with a seven-foot-tall hair-covered creature just north of the Everglades. One year later, a "large, hairy animal" reportedly killed and ripped apart a horse and beheaded a calf on the farm of Debbie and Michael Polenek in central Florida. An investigation revealed that tracks around the slaughtered animals resembled those of Bigfoot, or Sasquatch, the name given by the Indians to the creature.

Stories about fantastic creatures roaming the backwoods of North America are nothing new. Early pioneers pressing into the wilderness from the East Coast told of hair-raising encounters with giant bears, bear-men, wolf-men, and similar creatures. One of the most widespread legends, which probably had its origins in Indian mythology, centered on the "Wampus Cat," an impossibly hideous critter said to have the head of a man, the body of a wildcat—only larger—and the soul of a demon.

Like Bigfoot, the Wampus Cat was said to lurk among the gloomy river bottoms of the South and to take fiendish delight in preying upon hunters, fishermen, and others who strayed too far off the beaten path. Whereas Wampus Cat stories eventually petered out around the turn of the century, however, tales of harrowing run-ins with Bigfoot creatures continue to this very day.

Along the Mississippi River, and all across the arc of the Gulf Coast, numerous legends still exist about another dangerous creature, one the Cajuns call "Loup-garou." Half-man and half-beast, these hairy bipeds—which bear a remarkable resemblance to the Wampus Cat—are thought to be responsible for kidnapping children and livestock. In all, more than thirteen states, many of them southern, have reported sightings of incredible beasts such as Bigfoot, Loup-garou, or the Lizard Man.

As soon as stories about Lee County's own "Bigfoot" made the network news, it was only a matter of hours before curiosity-seekers swarmed into town. Along with the visitors came more sightings of the creature, which soon started being officially billed as the "Lizard Man" because of its reptilian characteristics.

A few days after Davis's initial sighting, another Lee County citizen reported shooting something that resembled the boy's description. The fellow even offered the local sheriff some scales and blood for proof. That proof, however, resulted in the shooter's receiving a citation. A crime lab analysis revealed the scales and blood apparently came from a dead fish.

Another couple camped near the swamp blamed the critter for battering their car and pulling wires out of the engine. That same day, a carload of visitors from Charleston claimed to have spotted a "large, ugly, gorilla-like thing" scurrying across a field about six miles from Bishopville.

In spite of the testimony from several respected eyewitnesses, local authorities continued to dismiss the Lizard Man as a hoax. Wildlife biologists called in to study a set of plaster casts made of the creature's footprints determined that at least some of the tracks were man-made. Those results, plus additional laboratory findings on what was said to be the creature's hair, worked to quiet the "lizardmania" that had swept through this small farming community of 3,500 people. Law enforcement officers, weary from answering calls at all hours

131

of the night from frantic citizens claiming to have spotted the creature, were relieved when things settled down a few months later.

But late at night, when the moon is high and a curious kind of silence stalks the clammy darkness, folks around these parts have become accustomed to thinking twice before getting in the car and driving through Scape Ore Swamp.

"Thou Shalt Take Up the Serpent!"

THE RITUAL BEGINS with a medley of old-timey preaching and gospel singing, followed by prayer and a round of frantic hand-clapping. Then, as the preacher walks down the aisle, sweat dripping profusely from his furrowed brow, chanting men and women in the packed congregation begin to sway.

With eyes closed and teeth clenched, the minister reaches inside a wicker basket and slowly withdraws a large rattle-snake. The audience gasps, responding in a raw chorus of "Hallelujah!"

The chanting subsides as the preacher, a stocky man in his late fifties, reaches into another box and pulls out a tangle of dark, hissing coils. Draping the venomous reptiles across his shoulders, he closes his eyes and lifts his head heavenward.

"Thou shalt take up the serpent, and neither fire nor harm shall come to thee." The sound of his voice bellows above the weeping crowd.

At that point a hysterical shudder sweeps through the rows of mostly middle-aged and elderly men and women, and eager hands reach out to fondle the poisonous swirl of rattlesnakes, cottonmouths, and copperheads clutched between the preacher's outstretched arms. In the front row, a woman dressed in a flower-print dress leaps from the pew and begins jerking violently, her slender arms twitching around in circles.

As if on cue, other members of the congregation follow suit, and above the impassioned strains of "Praise Jesus!" and "Amen!" they start speaking in tongues—high-pitched, rapid-fire bursts of incoherent exclamations. Cymbals clash, tambourines jangle, and a foot-stomping choir commences with a resounding rendition of "Nearer My God to Thee."

For the fifty or so members of Dolley Pond Church of God With Signs Following, it's just another Sunday night in Grasshopper Valley, Tennessee. The hour-long service will end with more shouting and the usual healing ceremony as backaches disappear and unneeded wooden crutches are cast aside. By the time the last stanza of "Just As I Am" is sung, the hysteria will have passed, and the dangerous snakes will return to their baskets and boxes to await the next meeting.

The Right Reverend George Went Hensley knows it's been a good night, and he smiles as the congregationists file past, offering spirited handshakes and hugs. As the church's controversial founder and spiritual leader of the southern snake-handling cult, Hensley has come a long way. In spite of jail cells, threats, fasts, and hundreds of snakebites, Hensley has catapulted his unique brand of evangelism into the nation's limelight.

On this particular night—January 14, 1945—Hensley is undoubtedly the most talked-about evangelist in the southern foothills of Tennessee. From his tiny church here in Grasshopper Valley, the minister has spread the word far and wide, claiming converts from as far away as Florida and the Midwest.

It had all happened so fast—almost like a dream, he would later recall. And Hensley—the Right Reverend George Went Hensley, as he insisted on being called—never missed an opportunity to talk about that dream.

The vision had come to him on a lonely mountaintop in east Tennessee one hot summer day in 1906. For years, young Hensley had been puzzled by certain scriptures in the Bible. Particularly troublesome was a passage in the Book of Mark, verses 17 and 18, which read, "And these signs shall follow them that believe: In my name shall they cast out devils; they shall speak with new tongues; they shall take up serpents; and if they drink any deadly thing it shall not hurt them; and they shall lay hands on the sick, and they shall recover."

Jesus had spoken these words shortly after the Resurrection and before the Ascension. As Hensley pondered their meaning, a vague idea for putting his faith to the test began to take shape in his mind. Suddenly, pieces of the eternal puzzle of life and death came together. All it involved was a literal interpretation of the scripture as written by St. Mark. In a blinding flash of inspiration, he walked across the mountain until he found a rattlesnake sunning on a rocky ledge. Trembling, but resolute in his determination to stare Satan down, he picked up the snake.

Convinced it was his faith that protected him, Hensley marched down the mountain with his rattler. His first stop was at a local evangelical prayer meeting where he feverishly related his revelation to friends and neighbors. At first the group was skeptical, less than inclined to allow a dangerous serpent into their church, let alone handle the thing.

After repeated demonstrations, however, and readings from St. Mark, a few bold members reached out and touched the viper. Instant jubilation exploded in the aisles as the hardscrabble assembly of dirt farmers, factory workers, and mill hands realized that God's power stood between them and the serpent's deadly fangs. A new American religion was born.

In the years that followed, hundreds of rural churchgoers converted to Hensley's bizarre form of worship. Snake-handling soon became a common practice at small churches, private homes, and wooded gatherings throughout backwoods regions of the Bible Belt. In his book *They Shall Take Up Serpents,* Weston La Barre describes such a meeting, based on a newspaper story filed by the *St. Louis Post-Dispatch:*

> The snake-handling lasted about half an hour, but the service went on for an hour or more. To the singing of such songs as "Jesus Is Getting Us Ready for the Great Day," several female communicants, eyes shut, hands waving, . . . moved their feet in a rhythmic step and wheeled slowly in backward circles. Frequently their bodies would jerk as if the spine were being snapped like a whip.

Some of the men also performed this jerk. Fire-handling by male saints was also performed; their hands, held in the flames of a kerosene torch and a miner's acetylene lamp, were blackened by smoke but otherwise appeared unhurt.

The rattlesnake cult was still largely unnoticed by the outside world. Michael Jenkinson, who investigated the snake-handlers in his book, *Beasts Beyond the Fire,* attributes this fact to the worshippers' relative isolation, rather than to some deliberate desire for secrecy.

By the 1930s, the use of rattlesnakes in church services had spread into several neighboring states. Virginia, West Virginia, Kentucky, the Carolinas, Georgia, Alabama, and Florida all reported snake-handling activities, usually in remote pockets away from the ridicule of bigger churches and the long arm of the law. Most people who attended these services were deeply religious and undoubtedly sincere in pressing their faith to the prescribed limits. However, the congregations must have included at least a few skeptics, curiosity-seekers, and even detractors.

In the early 1970s, the sheriff of Berrien County, Georgia, told a local newspaper that the cult had a "wide number of followers" in his territory as well as in nearby counties. Sheriff Walter Gaskins recalled an instance in the mid-1960s when a local pastor had been tried for murder after a snake bit a worshipper. The sheriff grimly told of other instances where "ignorant people" had been fatally struck while handling snakes at rituals.

In 1985 the pastor of a church in Cartersville, Georgia, died from the bite of a snake he had stroked during services. The pastor had refused medical treatment, believing until the end that the power of the Almighty would intervene and protect him from death. At his funeral, mourning members of the congregation explained that "God's will has been done."

The Cartersville pastor's death was only the latest in a long string of deaths and near-deaths linked to snake-handling. At least fifty persons had died either of snakebite or from drinking "salvation cocktails"—liquid laced with venom or strychnine, kept on hand in some churches in case a member felt compelled to make a particularly powerful statement about his or her faith. It is not known how many other deaths and injuries have gone unreported.

Some leaders will apparently go to any length to prove their belief in the power. When a young congregationist named Lewis Ford was fatally bitten by a rattlesnake at the Dolley Pond Church, the story was picked up by wire services and broadcast across the country. The pastor of the church, Tom Harden, saw in the tragedy a chance to advance his cult's cause. Jenkinson wrote,

> Now that his [Harden's] church was in the public eye, he saw an opportunity for gaining converts within the city limits of Chattanooga, which to the pious hill people was a fortress filled with all kinds of wickedness. Harden, accompanied by cult founder Hensley, set up a tent with an oil drum altar. Word got around. A curious crowd gathered and traffic was blocked. Harden and Hensley, to their delight, were taken to the city lockup. They likened their persecution to that suffered by the Biblical prophets.

While church members and other followers waited outside the jail to pray for their leaders, Harden and Hensley led inmates and jailers in singing spirituals aimed at driving out demons. The two men refused to pay a fine, insisting they had been called on to do God's work; their defiance won them a three-day stint on the local chain-gang pounding rocks.

Many snake cultists at that time viewed their leaders' release as "divine intervention," but the Tennessee legislature thought otherwise. A bill was soon approved outlawing the handling of venomous snakes during worship services. Other states soon followed suit.

Predictably, the new law did little to curb the illegal practice, which continued to flourish in out-of-the-way communities and hamlets from Arkansas to Kentucky. Authorities seemed caught between a rock and a hard place. On one hand, they were compelled by the court to arrest violators of the law; on the other, they were reluctant to impose restrictions on worship services, even though people continued to die from the fangs of serpents.

Today, the controversial rattlesnake cult of the Holiness Church and other denominational offsprings continues to thrive amid backwater draws of the Deep South, Midwest, and remote mountain regions of southern Appalachia. Despite dozens of snakebite deaths and crackdowns by the law, this strange religious practice appears to be a favorite among some fundamentalist churches whose communicants believe the Holy Spirit confers supernatural gifts, such as the ability to speak in tongues and to heal by prayer, the laying on of hands, and anointing with oil. The exact number of snake-handlers is not known, since records are rarely kept. But some mainstream clergymen estimate that "thousands" of people risk life, limb, and persecution by law for the privilege of handling dangerous serpents at meetings.

Many states still provide snake handlers with a vague form of protection from legal interference. An amendment in Georgia's state constitution is typical of these go-easy laws: "No citizen shall be molested in person or property . . . on account of his religious opinions. . . . All men have the natural and inalienable right to worship God . . . according to the dictates of his [sic] own conscience and no human authority should in any case control or interfere with such rights."

There is no specific reference to snake worship in the United States Constitution, and many attorneys feel the law is so nebulous that a court would have a difficult time making cult services cease.

Mainstream clergymen generally show little tolerance toward snake-handlers, although opinions are mixed about where to draw the legal line. Most view the dangerous ritual as a "gross misinterpretation" of St. Mark's scripture. "They [the cultists] have taken literal words and fashioned their own meaning from them," is how one Methodist minister in Georgia put it.

But another pastor in Alabama said, "God didn't intend for such sensationalism and foolishness to come into the churches. . . . Handling snakes and drinking venom to express one's faith in Christ is ridiculous."

One is tempted to wonder whether snakes used during services have been "doctored" to render them incapable of striking. Studies provided by churchgoers and outside witnesses show that these reptiles are not drugged, de-fanged, or gassed to make them less dangerous. Nor are the snakes "trained" not to bite, as are some poisonous serpents in circus sideshows. The many bites suffered by worshippers over the years seem proof enough to dispel any lingering doubts about the danger of the snakes. Fatalities continue to occur, even among the most experienced leaders.

In 1951, Ruth Craig, a veteran handler, held a small service at her home in New Hope, Alabama. Midway through the meeting, she pulled a writhing rattlesnake out of a glass jar and proclaimed, "I'm going to handle the snake and anyone who doesn't believe had better leave." Minutes later the horrified crowd watched the large snake bite their leader four times in rapid succession on the arms and shoulder. She collapsed into a coma and died the next day.

Three years later, Reece Ramsey of Rising Fawn, Georgia, was struck on the side of the head by a large diamondback he was holding at an open-air service. The elderly cultist smiled when offered to be taken to a doctor, but refused, confident that the Lord's healing power would soon cleanse away the devil's venom now coursing through his veins. Ramsey strolled toward the preacher, staggered, then fell down in front of the altar. While the congregation sang "I'm Getting Ready to Leave This World," the old man died in the arms of the preacher.

In 1965, fifty-nine years after founding his controversial religion, George Went Hensley was the guest speaker at a small, open-air service in Altha, Florida. At seventy-seven, the preacher and prophet still moved easily before the packed crowd of wide-eyed visitors, casually fondling a small diamondback rattler draped across his forearm. He was happy to be there, he told the clapping congregation in his trademark baritone voice, happy to be among God's children and the devil's own tempters—a reference to the hissing mass of rattlesnakes writhing around inside glass cages near the altar.

About fifteen minutes later, just as he went to put the snake away, it reached up and struck him on the wrist. It was only a sting, and Hensley proudly waved the wounded arm around for the crowd to see.

"Nothing to worry about," he assured the crowd. "It's just Old Satan knocking on the Lord's heavenly door." The evangelist reminded the audience that snakebites were nothing new to him. Over the past four decades, he said he had been bitten at least four hundred times. God would bless this bite too, and the evil fluid would be sucked out by an angel's kiss.

He could already feel the angel's heavenly breath brushing against his skin as he put the snake back into its cage and closed the door.

A few minutes later Hensley's skin turned purple and began to swell. Excruciating pain racked his body and he found it hard to breathe. He lost his balance, stumbling to his knees, trying unsuccessfully to smile.

Silence descended like a pall over the small audience as they watched their leader struggle to regain his composure. Finally, a couple of men on the front row rushed to his aid.

But it was too late. The snake had struck hard, burying its inch-long fangs into the preacher's veins and squeezing out a full load of venom. Now that pool of "evil fluid" was sweeping through his paralyzed body toward his heart.

The next morning George Went Hensley, "God's own anointed disciple of serpents," went into shock and died.

Monsters of the Deep

IN THE SUMMER of 1962, Edward McCleary and three companions from Miami were skin-diving off the coast of Florida when they noticed a disturbance in the water behind them. Because of a fog rolling in from the open ocean, the men—all experienced divers—were unable to make out the long, shadowy form slithering through the dark waves toward them.

When they finally saw the beast approaching, it was too late. The creature struck swiftly, devouring one of McCleary's companions in a single gulp, then dragging the other two kicking and screaming to their deaths below the surface. McCleary survived the ordeal by scampering into the group's anchored cabin cruiser. For several minutes he watched in horror as the monster circled the small boat, its green eyes glistening and turtle-shaped head reared high above the foaming waves. It finally gave up, however, and sank beneath the surface, never to reappear.

Surprisingly, the tragic encounter between McCleary and the sea creature received scant attention from the news media. There were a few headlines, but officials theorized that a large shark, probably something in the range of a twelve-foot hammerhead, had attacked the men. The skeptics said that the divers might have paddled into the middle of a shark breeding ground or even a feeding frenzy. Ridiculous, argued McCleary, who to this day vehemently denies that allegation, insisting instead that it was some kind of sea monster that killed his friends and terrorized him that foggy summer day long ago.

Encounters between people and dangerous sea life are nothing new in the warm coastal waters of the South. Several species of killer sharks are known to thrive there, as well as barracuda, sting rays, giant jellyfish, and numerous other potentially life-threatening creatures such as eels, whales, oarfish, and groupers.

Rarely does a summer pass without at least one shark attack report, barracuda bite, or severe jellyfish sting. Fortunately, the likelihood of bumping into one of these predators of the deep is quite remote. And a sea serpent? What are the odds of running into one of these fabled fellows, so dreaded and feared by seafaring voyagers down through the ages?

Pretty high, if you ask Dr. Berard Heuvelmans, a Belgian zoologist who has spent a lifetime investigating and writing about the sea serpent phenomenon. In his classic study of the subject, *In the Wake of the Sea-Serpents,* Heuvelmans came up with 587 reported sightings of sea monsters between the mid-seventeenth and mid-twentieth centuries. Of these, he determined that 121 were vague or doubtful, and another 50 or so others were hoaxes, many identifiable by their excessive detail. (One overheated account described a 200-foot specimen sporting a bright green handlebar mustache; another gave precise coordinates placing the observer in the Libyan desert.) Another 50 looked like mistaken identities—a train of playing porpoises, a flight of skimming sea birds, a mass of seaweed, or, if the sighting was of a stranded, rotting carcass, a basking shark.

Heuvelmans settled with 358 sightings that he considered fairly reliable, based on a number of factors—the number of witnesses and their credibility, location, time of day or night, weather, and physical descriptions.

The zoologist, who spent ten years researching and writing the book, was able to pin down seven distinct types of sea serpents. Their "convenient, informal" names are: Long-Necked, Merhorse, Many-Humped, Many-Finned, Super-Otter, Super-Eel, and Marine-Saurian. Part of what makes

Heuvelmans's work so fascinating is his use of modern scientific methodology in collecting and evaluating data—data which he feels proves conclusively that sea serpents are real. "The existence of the sea-monster, commonly known as the sea-serpent, is no longer in doubt today," Heuvelmans quotes Professor Leon Vaillant of the French National History Museum as reporting in a scientific journal shortly after the turn of the century.

For centuries, tales about such creatures have circulated. In ancient times sailors voyaging into uncharted waters fought "many-armed hydras," while accounts of similar marine behemoths continued to be handed down by seamen during the Middle Ages. Hundreds of sightings of unknown sea animals infesting southern waters have been documented through the years, starting with the first Spanish explorers. Some Indian tribes living along the coast also believed that horrible water demons dwelled offshore. Vikings who sailed south more than a thousand years ago kept a constant lookout for dangerous sea monsters. Even early French and English explorers surveying coastlines from Louisiana to Virginia left records detailing bizarre encounters with large, serpentine denizens of the sea.

But it wasn't until the modern era, when newspapers and magazines started carrying written accounts in the early nineteenth century, that news of sightings and even attacks became common. In 1830, for example, a Charleston, South Carolina, newspaper carried this story about a sea serpent attack:

> Captain Deland with the schooner *Eagle* ran into Charleston on the 27th of March, from Turtle River, and with his crew is willing to confirm by oath the truth of the following declaration: On the 23rd day of March, at one o'clock A.M., at about a mile from Simons Bay, we perceived at the distance of about 300 yards a large body, resembling an alligator, which sometimes moved with the vessel, sometimes lay motionless on the surface.

Captain Deland . . . approached the animal, loaded a musket with a ball, and steered so that he approached it within 20 or 30 yards at a moment that it lay quite still and apparently careless. Capt. Deland aimed with great sagacity at the hindpart of the head, the only part that was just visible, and the ball . . . struck.

The ball apparently only grazed the creature, which "suddenly grew angry" and turned on the boat. First, the monster rammed the wooden vessel with its enormous head, then began smashing into the craft with its flat tail. The report went on to say that as soon as the men realized the reptile was about to attack them inside the ship, they scrambled to safety atop masts and below deck. Those on deck were able to view the creature at close range and later gave vivid descriptions of the monster as it thrashed furiously in the water, repeatedly charging the boat.

Later, when the threat was over, the men agreed the creature was "about 70 feet long, had a body as thick as a 60-gallon keg, was gray in color, eel-shaped, without visible fins and was covered in greenish scales." Some of the sailors also said the creature's back was "full of joints or bunches, the head and back resembled an alligator's, and the skull was about 10 feet long and as big around as a hogshead." A smaller serpent spotted undulating through the waters a small distance away had been chased off by a couple of marksmen.

When the ship finally limped into port, an inquiry was held to assess damage to the ship and to determine what manner of creature had attacked it. One official who attended the meeting later dismissed the incident as a hoax, claiming, "It is not the habit of the sea serpent to attack a ship after having been struck by a ball, but to plunge down and disappear."

Another bizarre creature washed ashore at St. Augustine, Florida, on December 1, 1896. The find was hailed by investigators, the media, and the public as final proof of the existence of sea monsters. A professor sent down from Yale University to examine the octopus-like specimen determined that it had weighed over six tons when alive and measured 25 feet around its middle, with 75-foot-long tentacles dangling from its thick, dark mass.

A story which appeared in the *New York Herald* on January 3, 1897, reported that the beast had been dead for some time when found, and that scavengers had mutilated much of its decomposed body.

> Its head was nearly destroyed, and only the stumps of two arms were visible. The body, as it lies somewhat embedded in the sand, is 18 feet long and about 7 feet wide, while it rises 3½ feet above the sand . . . the weight of the body and head would have been at least four or five tons. If the eight arms held the proportions usually seen in smaller species of the octopus, they would have been at least 75 to 100 feet in length and about 18 inches in diameter at the base.

A half-century later, on a fine December day in 1947, the Grace Line's *Santa Clara* was sailing off the North Carolina coast when the startled cries of a Third Officer pierced the air. Thinking something must be horribly wrong, fellow officers and mates rushed to investigate.

What they saw, undulating close astern, was carefully described in the following radio message: "LAT 34.34 N LONG 74.07 W 1700 GCT STRUCK MARINE MONSTER EITHER KILLING IT OR BADLY WOUNDING IT PERIOD ESTIMATED LENGTH 45 FEET WITH EEL-LIKE HEAD AND BODY APPROXIMATELY THREE FEET IN DIAMETER PERIOD LAST SEEN THRASHING IN LARGE AREA OF BLOODY WATER AND FOAM . . ."

The decade of the 1940s witnessed an upsurge of monster sightings, the largest number appearing along both sides of the Florida peninsula. One such group of sightings occurred near Clearwater and was reported in detail by the local newspaper. "Tales of a sea monster's tracks about Clearwater and the beaches increase," screamed the headlines after a set of strange tracks was found on a remote Clearwater beach.

As soon as news of the tracks broke, frightened citizens started complaining of being chased by a "sea creature–like thing" along the beach. One investigator who studied the tracks in the sand said they matched those made by unusual three-toed creatures he had once seen in the silt marshes of Cuba. The newspaper quoted the man as saying:

> This critter walks on his hind legs, leaving three-toed footprints. . . .It has a head similar to a crocodile, but a much shorter jaw. The critter has large teeth. I am convinced that the tracks found on the Clearwater beach are not those of a human prankster because where would you find a man with an eight-foot stride? And if a prankster were using stilts he would have to have about three times his own weight added to them to get the depth of the footprints found.
>
> Moreover, the tracks on the beach showed where their maker had upset the lifeguard stand in front of Everingham's Pavilion and left evidence that some large, rough-skinned animal had rubbed against the wood of the stand. That doesn't seem to be the work of a prankster.

Similar tracks were found on the beaches at nearby Dan's Island and Honeymoon Island. "From Tarpon Springs," reported the *Clearwater Sun,* "comes the unconfirmed story that a sponge boat crew battled over 12 hours with some large denizen of the deep recently when it attacked some of the boat's divers."

Later that year, four pilots flying together claimed they watched a marine animal wallowing in shallow waters near Clearwater. They said, "It had the shape of a hog, was over fifteen feet long, and moved in a clockwise direction." In an interview with the *Sun,* they said that the creature "was only a few feet off the north end of Clearwater Beach, and was easy to see because of the white, sandy bottom. We're positive that it was furry and its legs or flippers were white with the ends cupped like hands." The report again described the creature's head as "hog shaped."

The Clearwater creature remained in the news for several more months, attacking bathers and occasionally crawling onto beaches and frightening residents of the coastal community. A county highway patrolman dispatched to the scene of one attack found a "near-panic . . . among residents of that beach area north of the Indian Rocks Hotel by the appearance of a sea monster which chased one individual, identified as John Moore."

Then, in 1952, the Clearwater monster returned, causing considerable excitement throughout the state of Florida. Huge tracks were once again found on the beach, this time by a local Coast Guard Commander. About forty feet of deep tracks led from the water's edge to a low sea wall, prompting investigators to decide that whatever had made them weighed over a thousand pounds. Long rows of claw prints preceded each set of tracks, measuring one foot long and seven or eight inches wide.

One marine expert theorized that the tracks indicated the creature's legs were about a yard apart—too wide, it would appear, and too deep to have been made by an ordinary 200-pound man.

Strange, serpentine creatures have also been reported in the backwaters of tidal rivers and lakes in other parts of the South. One such creature was spotted several times in the Altamaha River near Darien, Georgia, several years back; a "long, green, snake-like critter" chased a woman along the banks of the Savannah River near Augusta, Georgia, in the late 1800s.

The deep waters of the South are filled with a variety of forms of life. As we probe the depths, who knows what creatures wait there?

The Devil's Brother
And Other Strange
Travelers

The Goat Man of Dixie

FOR OVER FIFTY years he traveled the lonely backroads of the Deep South: a whistling, happy-go-lucky vagabond who enthralled small-town youngsters from Virginia to Florida with his tales of adventure on the open road. His name was Charles "Chess" McCartney, but everybody knew the bewhiskered old man driving a team of goats as the "Goat Man of Dixie."

Clad in his familiar overalls, boots, and scruffy cap, the Goat Man would pull into town, unhitch his team of goats, set up camp, then proceed to entertain wide-eyed crowds with his yarns. Huddled around a campfire, he would often stay up all night spinning tales about life on the road. "Would you like to hear about the time that old panther chased me through the swamp?" he'd ask, drawing dramatically on a large black pipe while poking the flames of his campfire with a knotty stick. "Or would you rather hear about the gang of outlaws that got after me in Kentucky? Later, I can tell you about the Indians who came after my scalp, and about that old grizzly bear who wanted me for breakfast . . ." He could carry a tune too, and the crisp night air often rang with his deep, rich voice—a voice that some said seemed to echo out of a turpentine barrel.

At the time of this writing McCartney was rumored to be in his 108th year. Until he retired his scraggly team of goats and old wagon a few years ago, he was a familiar sight in Arkansas, Texas, Louisiana, Mississippi, Alabama, Georgia, Florida, the Carolinas, Virginia, Tennessee, and Kentucky. He also traveled in the North some, but found the warm climate and

150

"hospitable nature of southern folk" more to his liking.

So many stories have cropped up over the years about him that it is difficult to separate fact from fiction. Some accounts claim he is a self-made millionaire, with sizable estates and mansions strung out all across the country. Others contend he was once a Russian spy, sent over to this country to keep count of the number of automobiles and trucks on the highways. In the 1950s, one story circulating in some parts of the South was that the Goat Man was the son of a famous Civil War general, some said Robert E. Lee himself. Another version linked him with General Ulysses S. Grant. It was this alleged association with the famed Union leader that earned him the wrath of a group of rowdies in Alabama back in the late 1940s.

"I had just pulled into this small town near Selma—I can't remember its exact name—and had unhitched the goats and built up a big, roaring fire," the Goat Man explained, tugging at a long, mossy beard swirling around his thin face. "A group of young'uns recognized me and came over to hear some stories. Well, as soon as I mentioned a part about the fighting between the states, some adults walked over and started calling me Yankee names.

"I knew I was in trouble, for no reason, and had to get out of there fast. They yelled at me as I hitched those goats back up and threw some rocks and bottles as I rolled away. Fortunately, none of my goats got hurt that night."

The fact is, McCartney was born in the North, in Iowa, to be precise, some time before the turn of the century—he won't say just how long. At the time of this writing he lives with his son, Albert Gene, in a converted school bus along Highway 80 in rural Twiggs County near Jeffersonville, Georgia. They moved into the bus a few years ago after their two-room shack was destroyed by fire.

The goats are long gone, given to a zoo in Florida in 1979. But McCartney misses his animals, especially on winter nights.

"You see," he said, blowing into his crusty palms, "I'd sleep with my goats if it got real cold. If it was a fairly cool night, I might get between two or three. But if it got nasty cold, it might take four or more to keep me warm. My goats are the finest electric blankets I can find. The colder it gets, I cover up with more goats—thirty degrees is a one-goat night; twenty degrees is a two-goat night; and below zero is a five-goat night."

McCartney said that during his long years on the road he camped in every state on the continent and often journeyed to Canada and Mexico. His box-shaped wagon pulled by a team of twenty goats was much heralded in many a small town along the way.

Children gathered around the Goat Man's camp often saw him as some larger than life hero, a rowdy, restless, rough-and-tumble adventurer whose pioneering spirit reminded them of Davy Crockett and Daniel Boone. Even adults who met McCartney in those years were awed by his wit, style, and story-telling ability.

Many people who knew the traveler idealized him, but others viewed him as a harmless old crank, a no-account drifter and potential troublemaker. Whenever it was rumored that the Goat Man was on his way to town, the sheriff would usually warn parents to keep a close eye on their children and valuables, just in case. "He's no better'n a gypsy," snarled one Tennessee lawman. "You have to keep a sharp eye out for the likes of these bums."

When the Depression hit his family's farm in Iowa during the 1930s, young McCartney decided to move south. Like many other Americans displaced by the economic crash, he became a hobo and soon learned how to profit from his misfortune.

He dressed in goatskins to draw a crowd during his travels, and soon found that people would flock around him to stare at his goats and even buy postcards he had made up. Along the way he met a woman, Saddie Smytheart, and the couple soon had a child, Albert Gene. Encouraged by the crowds—and the money they were willing to pay to see him—the Goat Man and his wife adorned their small son in goatskins and moccasins and had him pose for the people who swarmed around their caravan at every stop.

"I got the idea from Daniel Defoe's character, Robinson Crusoe," explained McCartney. "Dressing up the boy like that when he was just learning to walk was a real crowd-pleaser. It worked! They would buy our cards, and that money helped us work our way back and forth across this great country of ours, whenever and wherever we wanted to go."

But eventually Saddie Smytheart became weary of the rigors of the highway, and Albert Gene had to go to school. "This left me alone on the road with the wagon and the goats. Me and my team continued to go on, traveling here and there, far and near, always getting in trouble, but never having to go to jail."

In his heyday McCartney, who once preached the gospel as an ordained minister, was compared to another itinerant wanderer, Johnny Appleseed. The cheerful vagabond enjoyed that comparison, often remarking that he and the legendary Appleseed would have made a good team—"He a-doing the planting, and me a-doing the talking." McCartney estimated that he and his team of goats trekked more than 200,000 miles, camped at least 900,000 times, and burned "well over" a million junk tires to keep warm. In all that time, he never once slept in a bed nor in a house.

The old man tells of fighting off outlaws in Kentucky and California, Indians in Arizona and Texas, and a group of Ku Klux Klanners in Mississippi. Once he had to climb a tree to escape a grizzly bear in the Rocky Mountains. "I've met some mean hombres in my time—those that walk on two legs and those that walk on four," he said. "The ones that gave me the most trouble were up North. I ain't had a lot of trouble down here in the South. These are good people."

Nowadays, when he has to travel, the Goat Man goes by airplane or train. "It's a lot more comfortable. No use wasting what precious time is left in my life on a wagon."

And with his vagabond days behind him, the Goat Man—who says he's had four wives—wants to marry again and settle down.

"I'm gonna be around a long time to come. The devil ain't ready for me and the good Lord don't want me just now."

The Devil's Brother:
Blackbeard, Scourge of the Spanish Main

ABOUT THE ONLY good thing that could be said about Edward Teach, better known as Blackbeard the pirate, was that he was born an honest man. But a profitable lifestyle while privateering for the crown during Queen Anne's War probably convinced this swashbuckling rogue that it was easier—and more fun—to earn a living looting treasure and lopping off heads than working a regular job.

So, when the war ended in 1713, the greatest sea bandit of them all ceremoniously unfurled his black flag and launched his long and bloody career. In his day, Blackbeard captured or sank scores of ships, stole millions of dollars in treasure, took dozens of women as his wives, and left the mutilated bodies of thousands of victims who got in his way along the Atlantic coast from New England to Florida. But it is the memory of the pirate's treasure, more than his despicable deeds, that endures today. Although some of the loot has reportedly been found, untold fortunes in silver, gold, and jewels may remain buried beneath coastal sands, awaiting some lucky one's spade or metal detector.

Did Blackbeard himself leave any clues as to where his treasure was buried? It is said that on the eve of his last battle, one of Teach's henchmen questioned him about it. The pirate's swaggering reply was typical: "Nobody but the devil and myself know where my treasure is, and the longer liver of the two shall have it all."

Predictably, legends galore have sprung up about this formidable character. In real life he was an abnormally big man, but the impression he made on people was so much larger than life that some considered him to be the devil incarnate—a description he mastered at cultivating throughout his career on the high seas. Tall, well-built, and phenomenally strong, he wore a long, braided beard deliberately fashioned to unsettle friend and foe alike; according to tradition, the wiry swirls of luxurious growth covered every inch of his face, growing up to his eyelids and over his ears. Legend relates how he enjoyed setting off small charges of gunpowder in his beard that enveloped his head in a halo of black smoke. As a finishing touch to his satanic mien, he also drank his rum laced with flaming gunpowder.

A particularly gruesome example of Blackbeard's talents occurred shortly after he turned to pirating full-time, when his dreaded ship *Queen Anne's Revenge* came upon a commercial vessel off the Florida coast. First, his scruffy crew swung aboard the *Great Allan,* slew anyone who resisted, and grabbed the ship's supplies. After setting the ship ablaze, Blackbeard threw the remaining victims overboard in shark-infested waters. He is said to have roared with laughter as the sharks slashed into the helpless victims—men, women and children—and the sea turned red with blood.

On another occasion, he killed the fiancé of a woman he desired (reputedly the daughter of North Carolina Governor Charles Eden), cut off his hand, then presented the grisly gift to Miss Eden in a small silver casket. According to the story, the girl cried out in horror, fell into a swoon, and died within a month.

Soon after embarking upon his new profession, Blackbeard fell in with a certain gentleman pirate known as Major Stede Bonnet, a wealthy Southerner who had adopted pirating as a relief from boredom. The diabolical combination of talents resulted in a virtual wave of terror upon the high seas, with no port or sea lane safe from the double scourge. In two days alone they captured five vessels off the coast of Charleston, South Carolina, practically closing the port down. No captain in his right mind would take to the open water with the "devil incarnate" roaming the bounding main.

In his book *True Tales of Buried Treasure,* Edward Rowe Snow describes why many, including a number of his own crew, referred to Blackbeard as the very devil:

> One night soon after his successful exploits at Charleston, the pirate decided to give an exhibition of his Mephistophelean qualities. He took three of the more venturesome members of his crew aside, and, fixing his ferocious black eyes on them, told of his scheme. "Come," he roared, raising himself to his full height, "let us make a hell of our own and try how long we can bear it."'
>
> "All four men then descended into the hold." After Blackbeard had closed the hatches, he filled several large pots with brimstone and set them on fire. The four pirates remained in the cramped hold, breathing the suffocating smoke into their lungs until all but Blackbeard shouted for air. Then he released the hatches and allowed the others to pull themselves up on deck, not a little pleased that he had held out longer than any of his men.

Another illustration of Teach's particular brand of wickedness came when he tricked three hundred of his men into waiting for him on a small island. The marauding band of pirates had just returned from a profitable raid, and Blackbeard had promised them all their fair share of gold and silver bullion. Since the ship was overloaded with the ill-gotten booty, he told the men to wait behind, that he would return for them once the treasure had been safely deposited at a nearby hideout. After hand-picking a small crew to go with him, he waved goodby and set off, leaving the stranded men to their doom.

The strange relationship between Blackbeard and the North Carolina governor has tantalized historians for more than two centuries. Eden, an otherwise honorable man, apparently became involved with Teach after the pirate told him he had found several ships adrift at sea. The governor seems to have swallowed the story and, for a share in the booty, permitted the sea bandit to sail on his way.

On subsequent occasions, when Blackbeard sailed into port, Eden granted him full protection and even wined and dined openly with the cruel bandit. Some say Blackbeard had threatened to kidnap or murder the governor's young daughter unless he cooperated. Others claim the royal official was corrupt and had been in cahoots with the notorious pirate all along. Records show that periodically Blackbeard would sail into Bathtown to declare his intentions of going straight. On one occasion, Eden called together a Court of Vice Admiralty and arranged a full pardon for the villain's nautical crimes. The meeting was adjourned after Edward Teach had been declared an honest privateer again.

In North Carolina, rumors still persist that Teach had secretly been in love with the governor's daughter and that she helped him import piratical spoils into the Eden household for safekeeping. This was accomplished by means of a tunnel, supposedly leading from a secret harbor directly to the governor's mansion. Some historians dispute this theory, pointing out that Miss Eden would probably have been too young for the likes of Blackbeard at the time.

During Teach's long reign as the undisputed leader of the sea pack, other pirates, many of them equally fierce and successful in snatching unwary ships, roamed the sea lanes of the Atlantic between the Indies and New England. The thickly islanded coastal areas of Virginia, the Carolinas, Georgia, and Florida furnished excellent retreats for the buccaneers as well as homes for their stolen goods. José Gaspar (otherwise known as Gasparilla), Captain Kidd, Jean Lafitte, and Nasty Ned Lowe were among the dozen or so swashbucklers known to have cruised the area.

Nearly every coastal town and island has its own legend about buried treasure protected by phantom guards, usually in the form of bearded pirates armed with cutlasses and flintlock pistols. It is true that many secluded barrier isles along the Atlantic seaboard were visited by pirates and may still hide fabulous fortunes. It would have been easy for ships flying the feared skull and crossbones banner to slip unseen into tidal creeks, rivers, and inlets and dispose of their blood-stained booty.

One island in particular that stands out as a possible treasure dumping ground is Blackbeard Island, located a few miles off the Georgia mainland. Named after the notorious pirate himself, Blackbeard Island was known to be a frequent haven for Teach and his band of swarthy outlaws. Numerous local legends tell how Teach buried a king's fortune in gold somewhere amid the island's gloomy forests, planning to return one day to claim his illegal loot. Before departing the island, he appointed a young sailor to guard the treasure with his life.

Over the years, there have been reports of a headless ghost, pistols and knives tucked in a sash, wandering the beaches of Blackbeard Island.

In 1718 the British government decided it had had enough of the pirate. After posting a reward of one hundred pounds for his head, it dispatched a fleet of ships under the command of Captain Robert Maynard to hunt down and capture Blackbeard—or kill him, whichever seemed most expedient. Because Governor Eden of North Carolina could not be trusted to take action against his friend and former confederate, an arrangement was made for Governor Alexander Spotswood of Virginia to oversee Maynard's operation. At Ocracoke Inlet, thirty miles southwest of Cape Hatteras, North Carolina, Maynard's expedition finally caught up with its legendary quarry.

As Maynard approached Blackbeard's clearly marked vessel, the following conversation is said to have taken place:

Blackbeard: "Damn you for villains, who are you? And from whence come you?"

Maynard: "You may see by our colors we are no pirates."

Blackbeard: "Send your boat on board so that I might have a look and see who you are."

Maynard: "I cannot spare my boat, but I will come aboard

you as soon as I can with my sloop."

Blackbeard: "Damnation seize my soul if I give any quarter or take any from you!"

Maynard: "I expect no quarter from you, nor shall I give any."

In spite of his strong words, Maynard knew he and his men were up against the scourge of the Spanish Main, the most feared and ruthless pirate of all time, the man who had personally murdered hundreds of innocent men, women, and children in cold blood. He could expect no mercy from such a beast, nor should he allow himself to give any.

Maynard's hopes soared when he realized his enemy's ship had run aground in the shallow waters. Wasting no time, he tried to maneuver into a better position, angling toward a favored engagement of cannon. Unfortunately, just as the barrage was about to begin, the tide came in and freed the ship's murderous crew.

Teach was the first to attack. Without warning, a battery of cannons opened fire on Maynard, killing or wounding about thirty men. The desperate captain realized he was in a fight to the death and only trickery would get the best of this madman!

Quickly, the captain ordered most of the survivors to hide below the deck, to make their attackers think only a handful of sailors had survived the bombardment. As smoke swirled around the creaking deck and tattered canvas sails, Blackbeard's voice boomed across the narrowing waterway: "Look at 'em! Why, there's only three or four of 'em left alive! All the rest are knocked on the head. Let's jump aboard and cut the others to pieces. Let no one live to see the sunset!"

With a bloodcurdling whoop, he led a rampaging charge onto the smoke-filled ship. Quickly the hidden soldiers dashed out on deck, and a gory free-for-all ensued. Sabers clashed and knuckles cracked against bony flesh. Suddenly both captains spotted each other. Their eyes locked as they quickly drew their pistols and aimed. The crack of pistol fire was hardly audible above the roar of muskets and clattering of steel sabers. Seeing that both balls had gone wide of their mark,

Maynard and Blackbeard scrambled across the tilting deck toward each other, cutlasses swinging wildly.

In a flash they were upon each other, flailing with cleaver-like strokes of their swords. Blackbeard's heavier blade crashed against Maynard's smaller, regulation saber, shattering the flimsy metal down to the hilt. With a roar of demonic laughter, the pirate raised his blood-stained weapon high, preparing to decapitate the young captain with a single swipe. At that instant, however, a British comrade rushed up behind him and slit the pirate's grizzled throat.

That brave action slowed down the giant, but only for a moment. Staggering backward against the railing, Blackbeard regained his balance and took stock of the situation. Without hesitating any longer, he fell upon Maynard with a howling vengeance. Five more volleys of gunfire erupted over the ship, now littered with the bodies of dead pirates. Five steel balls slammed into Blackbeard, knocking him backwards and into the slashing swords of government seamen.

Edward Teach, riddled with bullet holes, was dead.

Not taking any chances, Maynard grabbed a sword from one of his men and cut off the pirate's head—proof that Blackbeard had at last been conquered. Without ceremony, his crumpled body was thrown overboard to the sharks.

And what about Governor Eden, Teach's partner in crime?

As soon as Captain Maynard reached shore, he marched up to the governor's house, confiscated a considerable quantity of stolen goods, and placed Eden and his staff under house arrest. However, the crafty governor managed to withstand the storm of adverse publicity that followed and remained in office. Fourteen of the captured pirates were hanged; a few were pardoned, including Israel Hands, Stevenson's character in *Treasure Island,* who sailed back to England and spent the rest of his life as a common beggar.

Blackbeard's "skull" continued to surface in taverns and fraternity houses in North Carolina and Virginia for a number of years. The grisly relic became a favorite among rowdy collegians who dared drink their beer from its gargantuan cavity. Some who have drunk from the skull claim to have been possessed with newfound vitality and strength.

Others who had trouble growing beards swore they soon sprouted luxurious new growths of thick, healthy hair swirling around their faces . . .

Is Napoleon's General Buried in North Carolina Grave?

IN A GRAVEYARD in the North Carolina backwoods, a moss-shrouded mausoleum towers over jagged rows of tombstones and simple wooden crosses. Its inscription, tarnished with time, reads: "In memory of Peter Stuart Ney, a native of France and soldier of the French Revolution under Napoleon Bonaparte, who departed this life Nov. 15, 1846, aged 77 years." Each year visitors flock to the tiny cemetery behind Third Creek Presbyterian Church in Rowan County to see the tomb of a man some believe was Marshal Michel Ney, the great French general who led the bloody winter retreat from Moscow to Prussia during the Napoleonic Wars in 1812.

But wait. Something seems to be wrong here.

What are the remains of an aristocratic French general doing buried in this remote North Carolina county, so far away from his homeland? More to the point, what are the remains of one of Napoleon's most famous commanding officers doing in America? Don't history books tell us that this romantic revolutionary died in a hail of musket balls, his white silk blouse drenched in blood, one cold, wet morning in Paris over 140 years ago?

And if that is so, and if the general's body is actually entombed in the French capital—in the Père la Chaise Cemetery, to be exact—then just whose remains are those in the North Carolina grave?

Answers to these and other questions have bedeviled scholars and local residents for decades. Ever since the arrival of a quaint schoolmaster in the early 1800s—a schoolmaster who spoke Hebrew, Latin, Greek, French, and English, just as General Ney did—things haven't been the same in this part of North Carolina. To begin with, many locals believe the strange schoolmaster was none other than the famous general himself, whom Napoleon called "the bravest of the brave" in reference to his successes as a gallant military leader. According to legend, the 77-year-old schoolteacher, who called himself Peter Stuart Ney, declared on his deathbed that he was indeed General Ney. An attending physician reported that the dying man raised himself up on one elbow and said: "By all that is holy, I am Marshal Ney of France."

One would think that such a confession would put an end to speculation over the schoolmaster's true identity. On the contrary, Ney's death touched off one of the South's greatest historical manhunts. Books have been written and scores of articles for international magazines and newspapers have appeared over the years as investigators, both serious and romantic, have probed the secrets of Ney's grave.

In 1887 Peter Stuart Ney's body was exhumed. Later, his handwriting was analyzed. After years of debate, historians, archivists, and medical specialists from Europe and the United States have yet to agree on their findings. As of this writing, it remains uncertain whether the rural schoolmaster was Napoleon's general—or a highly imaginative educator who delighted in impersonating the great commander.

Predictably, the controversy over the schoolmaster's identity continues to fuel debate among local residents as well as outsiders who come here to study the mystery.

"It's great fun," said Howell Boone, a historian from nearby Davis County who doubts that the scholarly schoolmaster had ever even been to France, let alone led the French army at Waterloo. "That's why the legend will probably never die. There will always be people who want to believe. There's genuine sentiment for the story." In Boone's estimation, Peter Stuart Ney was an educated Scotsman with a vivid imagination. Records do indicate that the dapper schoolmaster got carried away when in the presence of ladies or when drinking.

"When he had a bit too much of the local brew, he would insist he was Marshal Ney," Boone said. "I wonder if someone gave him a couple of stiff drinks when he was departing."

A few days before Christmas in 1815, eight months after Napoleon's abdication, General Ney swore allegiance to King Louis XVIII. When Napoleon escaped from the prison island of Elba, the patriotic general vowed to bring him back to Paris—"in an iron cage, if necessary."

As it happened, Ney had a change of heart. Instead of going after the former French emperor with sword and pistol, Marshal Michel Ney joined up with Napoleon, kneeling before him and pledging support. Napoleon's defeat at Waterloo resulted in Ney's capture and sentence of death by firing squad.

On the day of the general's much-publicized execution, however, legend has it that members of the firing squad used blanks instead of live ammunition. It is said that when the order to fire was given, Ney smashed a concealed bladder of pig's blood against his white shirt, to make it appear he had been shot. That night, according to the story, Ney fled Paris aboard a farmer's cart, disguised as a peasant. He didn't stop until he reached the coast.

One month later, on January 29, 1816, a man calling himself Peter Stuart Ney arrived in Charleston, South Carolina. Few records remain of this man's movement, but a few months later he turned up in Cheraw, South Carolina, then later in Lincolnton, Mocksville, and finally Cleveland, North Carolina, where he settled down as a schoolmaster.

There stories began cropping up about his shadowy background. They were inexorably linked to Peter Ney's impressive knowledge of the Napoleonic Wars and his intimate familiarity with French military affairs. He also followed events in Europe with more than passing curiosity. His handwriting was similar to the French general's, and both had scars from sword and bullet wounds in the same parts of the body. Perhaps the most convincing evidence associating the schoolmaster with General Ney was the man's willingness—even eagerness—to proclaim himself one and the same person.

Today, more than 140 years after the death of Peter Stuart

Ney, many questions remain unanswered. One of the most puzzling is why, assuming the legend to be based on fact, the general chose a remote hamlet in North Carolina as his refuge. Accustomed as he was to high living, why didn't he go to New York or Charleston or Boston or some other major cultural center of the New World as did many other European refugees of the period? Why did he take a low-paying job as a school-master in a tiny town off the beaten path?

Some say he took the job for reasons of security—that too many enemies had immigrated to larger American cities and that discovery of his true identity would have resulted in his immediate assassination. John David Ramsey, an archivist at Davidson College, said Peter Stuart Ney's decision to settle in the rural South suggests he might have been looking for a low-profile existence. "There's no question he was very intelligent and a well-educated individual," Ramsey said. "He could have been a Harvard University professor."

But he chose to spend the remaining years of his life in relative obscurity, subsisting in a lonely little backwoods town on the edge of the frontier, rather than risk an assassin's bullet. Still, every now and then the old urge to become "General Marshal Michel Ney" would erupt and Peter Stuart Ney found himself talking about his old life—usually over drinks in the local tavern.

Immigrant Scot schoolmaster or renegade revolutionary general—who is the real person buried beneath the six-by-twelve-foot brick mausoleum looming over the tiny graveyard behind Third Creek Presbyterian Church? James W. Wall, a historian from nearby Davis County, said the mystery proba-bly will never be solved. "I don't see how it can be," he said. "There's compelling evidence both ways."

Afterword

When I began this book in the spring of 1988, my primary objective was simple—to research and write about some of the Deep South's most famous and enduring mysteries.

As the project unfolded, however, I found myself drawn more and more to some of the lesser-known riddles that have befuddled and bedeviled generations of Southerners. So instead of rehashing traditional material, I chose to focus on some of the myths, tales and unexplained incidents that, for one reason or another, have all but been forgotten.

For example, few folks outside the Carolinas have ever heard of the "Carolina bays"—thousands of curious depressions in the ground believed caused by a giant meteor shower thousands of years ago. To me, this lack of awareness seems incredible since the origin of the bays looms as one of the greatest unsolved mysteries in modern science. And speaking of mysteries, the spectacular Surrency haunting at the turn of the century left thousands of journalists, scientists and clergymen from all over the world scratching their heads, yet little information about this phenomenon survives today.

Just about everybody has heard of the mound-builders, a mysterious, half-mythological race of Indians that supposedly disappeared centuries before the arrival of Europeans in the fifteenth century. Few people know, however, that "moon-eyed white men" supposedly walked the North American continent thousands of years ago, or that a wandering band of Welsh explorers led by the enigmatic Prince Madoc roamed the Southern hinterlands long before the arrival of Christopher Columbus.

Do mermaids exist? Does a Bigfoot-like creature stalk the wilds of Gulf Coast regions and more remote elevations of the Southern

Appalachian Mountains? Did a sea serpent somehow slither onto a Florida beach a few years ago and chase a crowd of terrified bathers?

Before we dismiss these reports as the products of pranks or the ravings of wildly disturbed imaginations, let us remember that many witnesses to these phenomena were respected members of their community—doctors, lawyers, airline pilots, police officers, clergymen and college professors—people who had everything to lose and nothing to gain by going on record with their claims. Untold millions of Americans, including at least one President of the United States, have reported sighting Unidentified Flying Objects; yet, the Air Force discounts such sightings, saying they are nothing more than hot air balloons, swamp gas, "Venus Ascending," or other atmospheric illusions.

What, then, are we to make of these mysteries? It depends, I suppose, on our own perspective. For scientists, concerned as they are with facts and an uncompromising search for test-tube truth, most of these great Southern mysteries loom as nothing more than fantasy. But for others, examining our mysterious past often leads to romantic conclusions about forces and events that, rational or not, seem to at least satisfy some of the primal wonder within us all.

It's good to think that most of these mysteries will never be solved. It's good to think there will always be a Wampus Cat lurking in the shifting shadows, or that one day divers probing the storm-tossed depths of the ocean will come upon the gleaming columns of ancient Atlantis. Mysteries, fortunately, will always be with us. Ever since we crawled out of the cave, there's always been something just beyond the flickering firelight to capture our attention, to arrest our imagination, to keep us guessing, to stir us on toward discovery. In an age of electronic marvels, it gives me a profound sense of ease to know there are still some things a bleeping computer screen can't solve.

As a child growing up in south Georgia, I was fascinated by tales handed down by the oldtimers. So intrigued was I by stories of rattling chains, red-eyed apparitions at the window and other terrifying encounters with the unknown, that the memories still linger, fresh and powerful, more compelling, in a sense, and real than before. Sadly, too many of these stories are disappearing at an alarming rate. Once gone, the knowledge of our people as a whole will be somehow diminished. Preserving the lore of the past, however spectacular and speculative, will only make us richer and wiser, insuring that generations to come will not be shortchanged of their heritage.

That's the main reason I wrote this book, I suppose—to help keep alive the speculation, the wonder, the flickering embers at the back of the cave. To me, the book has been a richly rewarding experience, a kind of nostalgic journey into a universe of forgotten truths—a universe teeming with quivering secrets, shrouded legends and historical black holes.

Some of these stories are spinoffs of articles I wrote for newspapers and magazines over the years. As such, they are for the most part objective in style. A few, however, are purely speculative, based on evidence gleaned from hundreds of interviews, journals, newspapers, diaries, magazines and official records. I have resisted the temptation to draw conclusions on most matters, preferring to let the reader make up his or her own mind.

—E. Randall Floyd
Augusta, Ga.
June, 1989

Bibliography

Adler, Bill, ed. *UFO's.* New York: Dell Publishing, 1967.

American Heritage Books. *Mysteries of the Past.* New York: American Heritage Books, 1977.

Aymar, Brandt. *Treasury of Snake Lore.* New York: Greenberg, 1956.

Barron, Ruth T. *Footprints in Appling County.* Dallas: Taylor Publishing Co., 1981.

Benwell, Gwen, and Arthur Waugh. *Sea Enchantress.* New York: The Citadel Press, 1965.

Berlitz, Charles. *The Bermuda Triangle.* New York: Doubleday & Company, 1974.

Blum, John M. *The National Experience.* New York: Harcourt Brace Jovanovich, 1973.

Bolton, Herbert E., ed. *Arrendondo's Historical Proof of Spain's Title to Georgia.* Berkeley: University of California Press, 1925.

Botkin, B.A. *A Treasury of Southern Folklore.* New York: Bonanza Books, 1967.

Bray, Warwick M., and Earl H. Swanson. *The New World.* New York: E.P. Dutton, 1976.

Brookesmith, Peter. *The Power of the Earth.* London: Orbis Publishing, 1984.

Bushnell, Geoffrey Hext Sutherland. *The First Americans.* New York: McGraw-Hill, 1975.

Capps, Clifford S., and Eugenia Burney. *Georgia.* Nashville: Thomas Nelson, Inc., 1972.

Carrington, Richard. *Mermaids and Mastodons.* New York: Rinehart & Company, Inc., 1957.

Carter, Samuel III. *Kingdom of the Tides.* New York: Hawthorn Books, 1966.

Cate, Margaret Davis. *Our Todays and Yesterdays.* Brunswick, Georgia: Glover Brothers, Inc., 1972.

Ceram, C.W. *The First America.* New York: Harcourt Brace Jovanovich, Inc., 1971.

Cottrell, Leonard. *Lost Worlds.* New York: Dell Publishing, 1962.

Courlander, Harold. *A Treasury of Afro-American Folklore.* New York: Crown Publishers, 1976.

Crane, Verner W. *The Southern Frontier (1670-1732).* New York: W.W. Norton and Company, 1981.

Daniken, Erich von. *Miracles of the Gods.* New York: Dell Publishing, 1975.

Davis, Nigel. *Voyages to the New World.* New York: William Morrow and Company, 1979.

Day, A. Grove. *Coronado's Quest.* Los Angeles: University of California Press, 1964.

Del Ray, Lester. *The Mysterious Earth.* New York: Chilton Company, 1961.

de Camp, L. Sprague. *Lost Continents.* New York: Dover Publications, 1970.

Dobie, J. Frank. *Rattlesnakes.* Boston: Little, Brown and Company, 1965.

Erdoes, Richard, and Alfonso Ortiz. *American Indian Myths and Legends.* New York: Pantheon Books, 1984.

Fell, Barry. *America, B.C.* New York: Demeter Press, 1977.

Grumley, Michael. *There Are Giants in the Earth.* New York: Doubleday & Company, 1974.

Halliday, William R. *Depths of the Earth.* New York: Harper & Row, 1966.

Heuvelmans, Bernard. *In the Wake of Sea Serpents.* New York: Hill and Wang, 1969.

Hill, Douglas, and Pat Williams. *The Supernatural.* New York: Signet Books, 1965.

Hudson, Charles. *The Southeastern Indians.* Knoxville: University of Tennessee Press, 1976.

Jackson, Donald Dale. *Underground Worlds.* Alexandria, Virginia: Time-Life Books, 1982.

Jenkinson, Michael. *Beasts Beyond the Fire.* New York: E.P. Dutton, 1980.

Jennings, Gary. *The Killer Storms*. New York: J.B. Lippincott Company, 1970.

King, Edward. *The Great South*. Baton Rouge: Louisiana State University, 1970.

Kirkpatrick, F.A. *The Spanish Conquistadores*. New York: World Publishing, 1971.

Klauber, Laurence M. *Rattlesnakes*. Los Angeles: University of California Press, 1982.

Kusche, Lawrence David. *The Bermuda Triangle Mystery—Solved*. New York: Harper & Row, 1975.

La Barre, Weston. *Thou Shall Take Up Serpents*. Minneapolis: University of Minnesota Press, 1962.

Mahan, Joseph. *The Secret: America in World History Before Columbus*. Acworth, Georgia: Star Printing Co., 1985.

Morison, Samuel Eliot. *The European Discovery of America: The Southern Voyages*. New York: Oxford University Press, 1974.

National Geographic Society. *Vanishing Peoples of the Earth*. Washington, D.C.: National Geographic Society, 1968.

Noone, Richard W. *Ice: The Ultimate Disaster*. Atlanta: Astraea Publishing, 1982.

Ogburn, Charlton. *The Southern Appalachians*. New York: William Morrow & Company, 1975.

Oliver, James A. *Snakes in Fact and Fiction*. New York: The Macmillan Company, 1958.

Reader's Digest. *American Folklore and Legend*. Pleasantville, New York: Reader's Digest Associates, 1978.

———. *Mysteries of the Unexplained*. Pleasantville, New York: Reader's Digest Books, 1982.

———. *Mysteries of the Ancient Americas: The New World Before Columbus*. Pleasantville, New York: Reader's Digest Books, 1986.

———. *Strange Stories, Amazing Facts*. Pleasantville, New York: Reader's Digest Books, 1977.

Ribeiro, Darcy. *The Americas and Civilization*. New York: E.P. Dutton, 1972.

Riegel, Robert E., and Robert G. Athearn. *America Moves West.* Hinsdale, Illinois: The Dryden Press, Inc., 1971.

Savage, Harry. *The Mysterious Carolina Bays.* Chapel Hill: University of North Carolina Press, 1982.

Smith, Page. *A New Age Now Begins.* New York: McGraw-Hill, 1976.

Stokes, Thomas L. *The Savannah: Rivers of America.* New York: Rinehart & Company, 1951.

Sweeney, James B. *A Pictorial History of Sea Monsters.* New York: Bonanza Books, 1972.

Thorndike, Joseph, ed. *Mysteries of the Deep.* New York: American Heritage Publishing Co., 1980.

Time-Life Books. *Mystic Places.* Alexandria, Virginia: Time-Life Books, 1987.

Vanstory, Burnette. *Georgia's Land of the Golden Isles.* Athens: The University of Georgia Press, 1981.

Velikovsky, Immanuel. *Earth in Upheaval.* New York: Doubleday and Company, 1955.

Whipple, A.B.C. *Restless Oceans.* Alexandria, Virginia: Time-Life Books, 1983.

———. *Storm.* Alexandria, Virginia: Time-Life Books, 1982.

Willey, Gordon R., and Jeremy A. Sabloff. *A History of American Archaeology.* San Francisco: W.H. Freeman, 1974.

Index

173

American folklore from
August House Publishers

Favorite Scary Stories of American Children
Twenty-three shivery tales newly collected from children aged five to ten.
ISBN 0-87483-119-9, TPB, $8.95

The Oral Tradition of the American West
Adventure, courtship, family, and local color in traditional recitation.
ISBN 0-87483-150-4, HB, $23.50
ISBN 0-87483-124-5, TPB, $11.95

Classic American Ghost Stories
Two hundred years of ghost lore from the Great Plains, New England, the South and the Pacific Northwest.
ISBN 0-87483-115-6, HB, $16.95
ISBN 0-87483-118-0, TPB, $9.95

Ghost Stories from the American South
Over one hundred tales of the supernatural, drawn from Tidewater Virginia to the Lone Star State.
ISBN 0-935304-84-3, TPB, $7.95

Cowboy Folk Humor
Jokes, tall tales, and anecdotes about cowboys, their pranks, their foibles, and their times.
ISBN 0-87483-104-0, TPB, $8.95

Mexican-American Folklore
Legends, songs, festivals, crafts, customs, tales of revolutionaries and saints, and more.
Winner of the Border Regional Library Association's Southwest Book Award.
ISBN 0-87483-060-5, HB, $19.95
ISBN 0-87483-059-1, TPB, $12.95

Spanish-American Tales
The practical wisdom of Spanish-Americans in 28 eloquent and simple stories.
ISBN 0-87483-155-5, TPB, $9.95

German-American Folklore
The legacy of German immigrants to the United States.
ISBN 0-87483-036-2, HB, $19.95
ISBN 0-87483-037-0. TPB, $11.95

Native American Legends
131 legends from the Creek, Cherokee, Quapaw, Biloxi, Chickasaw and other Southeastern Indian nations.
ISBN 0-87483-040-0, HB, $19.95
ISBN 0-87483-041-9, TPB, $9.95

August House Publishers
P.O. Box 3223, Little Rock, Arkansas 72203
1-800-284-8784